Modern Stereogram Algorithms
for Art and
Scientific Visualization

A C++ Sourcebook

Timothy Masters

Great effort has been undertaken in ensuring that the content of this book, including all associated computer code, is as close to correct as possible. However, errors and omissions are inevitable in a work of this extent; they are surely present. Neither this book nor the associated computer code are meant as professional advice. No guarantee is made that this material is free of errors and omissions, and the reader assumes full liability for any losses associated with use of this material. The algorithms described in this book and implemented in the associated source code are my own versions and not vetted by outside experts or tested in the crucible of time.

About the author:

Timothy Masters received a PhD in mathematical statistics with a specialization in numerical computing. Since then he has continuously worked as an independent consultant for government and industry. His early research involved automated feature detection in high-altitude photographs while he developed applications for flood and drought prediction, detection of hidden missile silos, and identification of threatening military vehicles. Later he worked with medical researchers in the development of computer algorithms for distinguishing between benign and malignant cells in needle biopsies. For the last twenty years he has focused primarily on methods for evaluating automated financial market trading systems. He has authored many books on applications of predictive modeling:

Practical Neural Network Recipes in C++ (Academic Press, 1993)
Signal and Image Processing with Neural Networks (Wiley, 1994)
Advanced Algorithms for Neural Networks (Wiley, 1995)
Neural, Novel, and Hybrid Algorithms for Time Series Prediction (Wiley, 1995)
Assessing and Improving Prediction and Classification (CreateSpace, 2013, Apress, 2018)
Deep Belief Nets in C++ and CUDA C: Vol I: Restricted Boltzmann Machines and Supervised Feedforward Networks (CreateSpace, 2015, Apress, 2018)
Deep Belief Nets in C++ and CUDA C: Vol II: Autoencoding in the Complex Domain (CreateSpace, 2015, Apress, 2018)
Deep Belief Nets in C++ and CUDA C: Vol III: Convolutional Nets (CreateSpace, 2016, Apress, 2018)
Data Mining Algorithms in C++ (CreateSpace, 2016, Apress, 2018)
Testing and Tuning Market Trading Systems (CreateSpace, 2018)

The software referenced in this text may be downloaded from the author's website:
TimothyMasters.info

ISBN 978-1719097406

Contents

1

Introduction to Stereograms

Our eyes use two different mechanisms to direct their attention to objects at different distances. One mechanism is *focus*. Muscles in the eye adjust the focal distance of the lens such that the object we are observing has perfect focus on the retina. The other mechanism is *convergence*. If the object is far away, both eyes point almost straight ahead, while if the object is close the eyes point inward so that they are both pointing directly at the nearby object. Normally, these two mechanisms work in perfect harmony, agreeing with each other on the distance to the object. But with a little practice, most people can decouple these actions and thereby see an object in stereo, with impressive depth perception, while looking at a single image. Because only one image is needed to achieve stereo perception, such images are usually called *single-image stereograms*. There are other types of stereograms, but they are beyond the scope of this text.

To understand the essential theory behind single-image stereograms, look at Figure 1 on the next page. The vertical line in the middle of the figure represents a viewing surface, which may be something transparent such as a pane of glass, or a computer screen. An object with varying depth (distance from the eyes and viewplane) appears on the right side of the figure. Consider a point on this object being seen by both eyes. The left eye will see this point at location *A* on the viewplane, while the right eye will see it at location *B*.

Suppose the viewplane is an image such as a printed graphic or a computer monitor. If we can somehow induce the eyes to focus on the viewplane while simultaneously converging behind the viewplane, and if we make points *A* and *B* identical (the same color), we can fool the brain into thinking it is looking at a point on the surface of an object behind the viewplane.

Unfortunately, things are not this simple. Look at Figure 2. Point 1 on the object requires that points *A* and *B* on the viewplane be identical. But point 2 on the object requires that points *B* and *C* on the viewplane also be identical. Point *B* is acting as a bridge, connecting more distant points on the viewplane. The result is that we end up with a multitude of constraints that must be imposed on the colors shown on the viewplane.

This is not a trivial undertaking, as will be seen later when the software algorithms are presented. But in most reasonable situations it can be done, and the results can be spectacular with good software in the hands of an artist. This book will document software for implementing the most important single-image stereogram algorithms, present complete source code for the key components of these algorithms, and provide basic guidance in some of the most important artistic techniques.

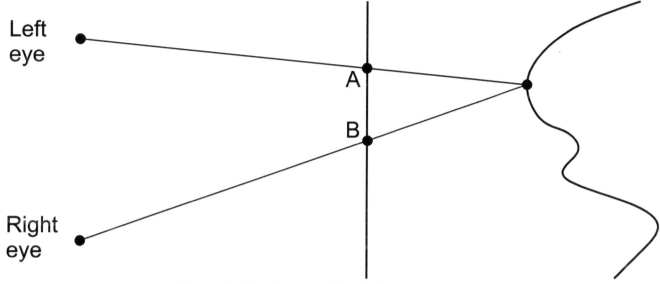

Figure 1: Simple case of single-image stereogram

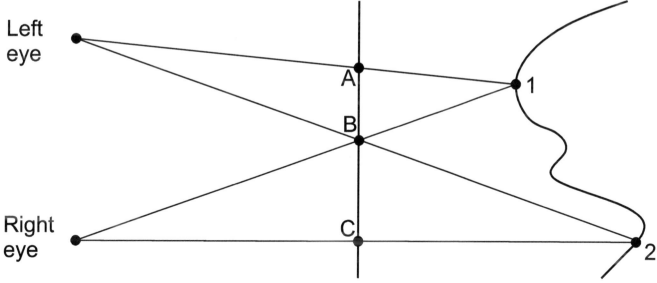

Figure 2: Chain constraints for a single-image stereogram

Visualizing a Stereogram

Describing how to visualize a stereogram is harder than explaining to someone how to ride a bicycle. Honestly, for the most part you just have to try until you get it. I have found that children tend to get it almost immediately, while elderly people often find it impossible. This is likely because the longer your eyse and brain have practiced coordination of focus and convergence, the harder it is to break that connection. Still, the rewards of using what I call 3D vision are well worth the effort.

In the interest of full disclosure, I should say that there are a few experts (perhaps I should put that in quotes) who claim that learning to decouple focus and convergence can have deleterious impacts on vision. I myself have never seen any even remotely convincing evidence that this is true, and to the best of my knowledge this is an extreme minority opinion. Still, you should be warned of this possibility and do your own investigation if you feel the necessity.

The most important point is that achieving 3D vision requires and is improved by practice. In the process of writing this book and creating numerous demonstration, I have reached the point of looking at a stereogram and seeing it in 3D almost instantaneously. Prior to this endeavor, when I just occasionally flipped through books of stereograms, it would usually take me several seconds for the effect to appear. Practice makes perfect, and once you have it you will never forget.

There are a few things that can make it easier. First and foremost, remember that your eye's lens must focus on the image, so if you require glasses to see things at the distance between your eye and the stereogram, you must wear those glasses. I myself am very nearsighted, so I have to remove my glasses. Before you can see the object in 3D vision, you must be able to *clearly* see the image on the computer display or printed page. Even slight blurriness can make it difficult, if not impossible, for even an expert to see the image in 3D. Also, viewing a printed page in a well lit environment helps by making it easier for your eyes to focus due to shrinking of the iris creating a greater depth of field.

Finally, and most reliable for beginners, is to draw a pair of dots side-by-side on the stereogram, spaced about 1.25 inches (half the average distance between eyes) apart. The *Stereo* program has this option. Look at these dots until you see exactly three dots. Concentrate on the middle dot, which will be most substantial because it is being seen by both eyes. Once you have this, which is the perfect 3D vision situation, slowly move your eyes away from the dots and onto the rest of the stereogram. It should appear in full 3D.

Other Stereogram Work

Stereograms have a history going back decades, or even centuries in their most primitive but still interesting forms. When mass-produced wallpaper came into fashion, certain patterns that repeated at exactly the right spacing were known to produce peculiar 3D effects when viewed with what we now call 3D vision, a visionary artifact not infrequently associated with a state of excessive drunkenness!

Several scientific papers were published on the subject, most notably "Automatic Stereoscopic Presentation of Functions of Two Variables" by Julesz and Miller, in *Bell Systems Technical Journal* Volume 41 in 1962. But the big practical breakthrough came when Thimbleby, Inglis, and Witten published *Displaying 3D Images: Algorithms for Single-Image Random-Dot Stereograms* in the October 1994 issue of *Computer* magazine. They presented an efficient and effective algorithm, along with computer code, for generating images containing random dots that followed the constraints implied in Figure 2, as well as handling other critical issues such as hidden surface removal. Images produced by their algorithm (which itself was strongly based on prior work) looked like a meaningless, patternless collection of dots. But when viewed with 3D vision, objects popped out of the screen or page in a dramatic depth dimension.

That paper, along with an article in the July 1995 *Dr. Dobbs* magazine, led to an outbreak of programs that produced single-image stereograms. Some were amateurish, while others were quite sophisticated. But the bubble burst in the late 1990's, and most remaining stereogram programs are unsupported or have completely vanished. An internet search will easily track down the few that remain.

Since then I have flirted with stereograms, and I have amassed quite a collection of stereogram books. The variety of stereogram books available is impressive; I have everything from *Bible Stories in 3D* to *The 3D Kama Sutra*. But my own personal breakthrough came when I discovered the phenomenal stereogram artwork of Gene Levine and Gary Priester. In particular, their *Startling Stereograms* is a work of pure genius. As I looked through this collection of true masterpieces, I kept asking myself, "How did they *do* that?" I soon learned that the secret is a technique called *Texture-mapped stereograms*. This is an extremely sophisticated set of algorithms in which the constraints can be strengthened in such a way that not only are the chain constraints of Figure 2 satisfied, but color assignments can be constrained in ways that map texture images to the stereogram. Alas, I also discovered that these algorithms are closely guarded secrets.

So I set about to figure out how it's done, and this book, along with its accompanying *Stereo* program, are the result. Enjoy.

2

Overview of the Stereo Program

File Menu Options

The following menu options are available:

Read Background Sprite

An image file is read for use as a background sprite. (Currently, only 24-bit BMP is supported.) This file will be used for sprite-based (including flat) stereogram generation. It is ignored for texture-mapped stereograms. To ensure best visual appeal, it is strongly recommended that it be horizontally periodic with a period of half the eye separation that will be used later for stereogram generation. In other words, in most situations its width will be exactly half the eye separation, and when one tile of it is placed beside another tile there will be no visible dividing line where they meet. This is not theoretically required, but failure to do this results in ugly discontinuities. Achieving this goal by generating a sprite of half the desired width, mirroring it, and stitching the original and mirrored copies together does satisfy this requirement, but the resulting symmetries are usually very obvious and ugly in the final stereogram.

If you will be overlaying a texture onto the sprite (Page 42) and hence have the sprite width equal to the stereogram width, this horizontal periodicity is still required internally for best appearance. For example, suppose your eye separation is 1000 columns. Then for every column in the sprite, its color should equal the color 500 columns to the left and to the right, and there should be no obvious vertical lines of discontinuity.

A flat stereogram (Page 31) will rescale the entire sprite image as needed, so the sprite width is arbitrary rather than needing to be half of the eye separation. But sprite-based stereograms will not rescale it, so you should make its width exactly half the eye width for best results, or else make it the entire stereogram width, and have internal periodic repetition. Making it anything else for a sprite-based stereogram is legal but will almost certainly give poor results.

In most cases, you will want to make its height (number of rows) equal to the height of the desired stereogram. If it is less, it will be tiled vertically, so you should ensure periodic continuity in the vertical direction as already discussed for the horizontal direction. Failure to do so will result in ugly horizontal lines of discontinuity.

The sprite will always be displayed in the lower-left corner of the computer monitor.

Here is a frequently good way to use an image editing program make a half-eye-separation sprite panel with periodic continuity. Create an image of the required dimensions (height equals the stereogram height, width equals half the eye separation). Create a nice pattern in the interior columns, but leave the outer 1/4 columns or so (roughly) blank. Split the image roughly in half vertically, move the right half to the left of the left half, and stitch them together. The interior is now blank. Fill it in. Voila.

Make Test Sprite

This creates a crude random sprite, not particularly pretty, but useful for testing. You must specify the dimensions. No periodicity is created, so vertical discontinuities will appear in a stereogram made from it.

Read Texture

A texture map image file is read. (Currently, only BMP is supported.) This must be the same dimensions as the depth map and final stereo image. If the purpose of this texture is to overlay onto a sprite, the sprite must also have these dimensions.

Texture maps are always 24-bit RGB. Pure black pixels (R=G=B=0) are considered background and ignored. The implication is that your texture object cannot have any pure black pixels! Inclusion of any pure black pixels in the object will result in weird and ugly results. In practice this is not a limitation, because one could use a tone that, to all appearances, is black but is not pure black. But it is an annoying detail to keep in mind when designing the texture image.

In most applications, for best results the horizontal extent of the object in each row (column of rightmost object pixel, minus column of leftmost) must not exceed the repetition distance given by Equation (5.2) on Page 104. Using NEAR as defined by Equation (5.3) on Page 106 as the limit is a conservative and simple test. A quick-and-dirty rough limit is about 1/3 the eye separation.

This limit applies separately to each row. Thus, it is possible to spread the texture across the entire width of the image. For example, one might have a central face near the top, a raised foot near the right of the image, and a foot on the floor near the left side of the image. As long as each individual row satisfies the limit, everything is fine.

Occasionally, you can violate this limit without bad results. An example is given on Page 48. In that example, single-object texture mapping is used to present an object composed entirely of narrow components. By careful design it can be possible to prevent ugly conflicts when the object has little to be in conflict. It is nearly impossible to safely violate this limit for any method other than single-image texture mapping. If you wish to violate this limit, you would be best off limiting the number of pixels in the object so as to limit the potential for clashes. The demonstration on Page 48 is a good example of how to produce a wide object with relatively few object pixels. Also, some distortion is inevitable. Thus, you should avoid objects for which even a few errors would be objectionable, a good example being faces or detailed images.

The texture image is always displayed in the upper-right corner of the computer monitor.

Read Depth

A file containing the depth map for the stereogram is read. (Currently, only BMP is supported.) If a texture is also used, the texture and depth images must be the same size, and the location of the object must be exactly the same in the texture and depth files.

The depth file must be 24-bit RGB. The blue and green channels must be equal, and this value determines the depth, with the red channel playing no role in depth determination. Pure black (0) maps to $Z=0$, the backplane, which is the furthest distance from the viewer. Pure white (255) maps to $Z=1$, the closest possible distance to the viewer.

For the two texture-mapped stereograms (single-object and multiple-object), the red channel of a 24-bit depth map is ignored, except for optional use as super-texture (Page 54). For a sprite-based stereogram, the red channel has a handy optional use. For each row (with rows handled separately and independently) the user may set the red channel of a single column as a flag. Values less than 128 are ignored; values greater than or equal to 128 are considered flagged. There is no point in flagging more than one column; if this is done, only the rightmost of them is considered flagged, and others are ignored.

When a sprite-based stereogram is generated, the optional flagged column is considered a center of importance. Whenever more than one sprite column competes to determine the color of a display column, whichever sprite column is closest to the flagged column is chosen. This facilitates imposing a texture map onto a sprite-based stereogram. For example, suppose one designs a sprite-based stereogram of a person, with the sprite dimensions the same as the depth dimensions. One could also create a texture map of the person's face, properly placed in conjunction with the depth map, of course. Overlay that face onto the sprite, and then, for each row of the face, set the red channel of the depth map for the center column of the face texture in that row. Thus, when the stereogram is generated, the face will appear in its proper place with respect to the rest of the person. This tremendously increases the realism of the stereogram, without revealing the entire person.

The same horizontal width limits apply to this use as those described in the section on texture maps. If, for any row, the width of the texture exceeds the limit, errors will occur for this row.

The depth image is always displayed in the lower-right corner of the computer monitor.

Make Depth Backplane

This is a quick-and-easy way to generate a depth file that has the same depth across every row but for which the depth changes a few times vertically. A typical use would be to generate a large backplane (Z=0) to represent sky at the horizon, and then at the bottom of the depth image rapidly change to Z=1 as a 'ground' platform. It could also be used to quickly generate a series of shelves on which objects could be placed.

The user is presented with two columns of seven rows each. The left column represents the percent (0-100) down from the top, and the right column represents the corresponding percent (0-100) of full depth. In particular, Z equals this value divided by 100.

Values in the left column must be in strictly ascending order, beginning with 0 and ending with 100. Blank rows are ignored. Change in depth is linear.

For example, suppose the following information were entered:

```
    0     0
   90     0
  100   100
```

Then the top 90 percent of the depth image would be at the backplane (Z=0). The bottom 10 percent would rapidly move forward, reaching Z=1 at the bottom row.

Depth From Function

The user is first prompted to enter the dimensions of the image to be generated. Then the user must select a text file that contains the function to be evaluated to define the depth image. The program will evaluate the function using X (horizontal) and Y (vertical) values ranging from 0.0 through 1.0 with origin at the bottom-left corner. The user must define a value Z as the last action taken. For each X,Y pair, the computed value of Z will define the depth. If the computed Z is outside the range (0.0, 1.0) it will be truncated to the appropriate limit.

The following operations are available. Logical operations always return 1.0 if true and 0.0 if false. Values not equal to zero are treated as true, and zero is false. Common priorities of evaluation are observed, with priorities as shown below. Operations are grouped with dashes (-----) from last evaluated to first evaluated. However, in case of doubt, parentheses are advised.

||	Logical: Are either of the quantities true?
&&	Logical: Are both of the quantities true?

==	Logical: Are the quantities equal?
!=	Logical: Are the quantities not equal?
<	Logical: Is the left quantity less than the right?
<=	Logical: Is the left quantity less than or equal to the right?
>	Logical: Is the left quantity greater than the right?
>=	Logical: Is the left quantity great than or equal to the right?

+	Sum of the two quantities
-	The left quantity minus the right quantity

----

*	Product of the two quantities
/	The left quantity divided by the right quantity
%	Both quantities are truncated to integers; the remainder of the left divided by the right
**	The left quantity raised to the power of the right quantity

----

-	Negative of the quantity
!	Logical: reverses the truth of the quantity

ABS( ) Absolute value of the quantity
SQRT( ) Square root of the quantity
CUBERT( ) Cube root of the quantity
LOG10( ) Log base ten of the quantity
LOG( ) Natural log of the quantity
POWER( ) Ten raised to the power of the quantity
EXP( ) Exponentiation (base e) of the quantity
ATAN( ) Arc-tangent of the quantity
LOGISTIC( ) Logistic transform of the quantity
HTAN( ) Hyperbolic tangent of the quantity
SINE() Trigonometric sine of the argument in radians
COSINE() Trigonometric cosine of the argument in radians

You can evaluate the truth of a logical expression and choose the execution path accordingly. This is done with the following expressions:

```
IF ( NumberExp ) {
    Commands executed if NumberExp is nonzero
    }

ELSE IF ( NumberExp ) {
    Commands executed if NumberExp is nonzero and all prior if expressions are zero
    }

ELSE {
    Commands executed if all prior if expressions are zero
    }
```

Note:

1) curly braces {} are required for all logical and looping operations, even if the operation encloses just one command.

2) Logical expressions may be nested.

Case (upper/lower) of all letters in the function definition file is ignored. All commands must end with a semicolon, except that the curly brace used to begin and end logic blocks is also a line terminator.

I do apologize that syntax error reporting is minimal. However, most user functions will be small and simple enough that syntax errors would be rare and easily debugged by trial and error if encountered.

Here is an example of a function that may be used to generate a depth image. The corresponding image is shown below.

```
AA = COSINE ( 6.0 * X * 3.141592653589793 ) ;
IF (Y < 0.5) {
   BB = SINE ( 8.0 * Y * 3.141592653589793  ) ;
   }
ELSE {
   BB = SINE ( -8.0 * Y * 3.141592653589793  ) ;
   }
Z = 0.25 * (AA + BB + 2.0) ;
```

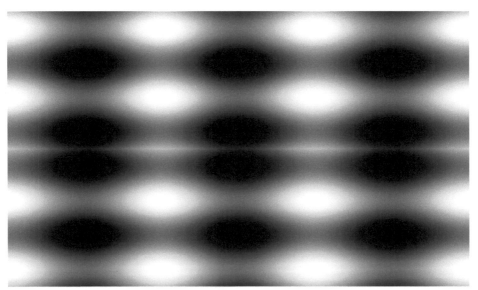

Figure 3: Depth file from the function shown above

Read Work1

An image file (currently, only 24-bit BMP is supported) is read and saved in the Work1 area, and displayed in the upper-left corner of the computer monitor.

Read Work2

An image file (currently, only 24-bit BMP is supported) is read and saved in the Work2 area, and displayed in the upper-center of the computer monitor.

Save Work1 Image

The image that is currently in the Work1 area is written to the specified file.

Save Stereo Image

The image that is currently in the stereo area is written to the specified file.

Print Stereo Image

The stereo image is printed. Two parameters must be supplied by the user:

> ***Percent of page width*** - Approximately this percent of the printed page width will be used. Remember that for easiest viewing, the number of columns specified for eye separation when creating the stereogram must be reasonably close to 2.5 inches (2-3 is usually fine) when printed.

> ***Vertical scaling percent*** - This allows the aspect ratio to be changed. For most printers, the default of 100 will produce square pixels.

Image Menu Options

Sprite Stereo Image

A sprite-based stereogram is computed and displayed in the bottom-center of the monitor. A sprite image and a depth image must be present. Typically, these images will be the same height (number of rows). If the sprite contains more rows than the depth, bottom rows will be ignored. If the sprite contains fewer rows than the depth, it will be tiled vertically as needed. In this case, it should be vertically periodic (the top of one tile merges smoothly into the bottom of the tile above) if ugly horizontal seams are to be avoided.

The column relationship nearly always falls into one of two categories In simple situations, the number of columns in the depth image is a multiple (not necessarily integer) of the number of columns in the sprite image, typically 4-8, with 5-6 being most common. Having less than a multiple of 4 makes visualizing the stereo image difficult or even impossible, while having more than 8 or so usually produces an unnecessarily large number of pattern repetitions, legal but often unappealing.

The number of columns in the sprite image is often called FAR as discussed on Page 103, and is half the eye separation in the simplest cases. For best visual appearance, the sprite must be horizontally periodic, meaning that when one instance of the sprite is placed beside another instance, the seam between them is invisible, with one instance blending smoothly into the next. Failure to follow this rule causes ugly vertical seams.

If the user will overlay a texture onto the sprite, then the number of columns in the sprite image must equal the number of columns in the depth image, with the texture placed in conformity with the corresponding location in the depth image. In this case, except for the (relatively narrow!) overlaid texture, the sprite should still be horizontally periodic with period FAR (half the eye separation), typically 1/8 to 1/4 of the number of columns, resulting in 4 to 8 smooth, seamless repetitions across the image. If horizontal periodicity is not present (lazy user!), then for each row the program will favor columns near any flagged columns (Page 42) if they are present, or near the center of the image if no flagged columns are present. This will result in a sort of periodicity that is theoretically enforced but not always pretty.

The generated stereogram will have the same dimensions as the depth image.

The following information must be supplied by the user:

Eye spacing - This is the number of columns separating the viewer's eyes. It is an extremely critical quantity. Most people's eyes are about 2.5 inches apart, so when the stereogram is printed or displayed for viewing, it should be scaled so that this many columns map to about 2-3 inches. Recall that the sprite, if used, has periodic horizontal repetition. In nearly all cases, it is important that *the eye spacing be exactly twice this repetition period*. Failure to follow this rule will usually result in minor to major discontinuities that will negatively impact the appearance of the stereogram. Also, making the eye spacing any more than about half the total width of the stereogram will make visualization of the stereo image difficult, although exactly half is usually acceptable. Dropping it to about 1/3 the stereogram width is often nearly optimal. Most demonstration stereograms in this book have an eye spacing about 1/3 the total image width, resulting in 6 repetitions of the background sprite. Because the images are 7 inches wide, the eye spacing is 7/3=2.333 inches.

Alignment dots to aid focus - People unaccustomed to viewing stereograms may be aided by the inclusion of a pair of focus dots. The person would adjust their eyes until the two dots align in such a way that exactly three clearly defined dots appear. This is the eye alignment that is perfect for viewing the stereogram.

Oversampling rate - For rapid experimentation and confirmation of quality, this should be left at its default of 1. If it is set to a value greater than 1, each row is stretched out into the original number of columns times this quantity. Computations are done on this extended row, and then the final stereogram is computed by averaging the tones in each oversample group. This is extremely beneficial, as it reduces or even eliminates (if oversampling is large enough) anomalies due to rapid depth changes. The need for oversampling depends on the presence of sudden large changes in depth.

Show unconstrained - This is a strictly diagnostic tool. In practice this would always be left at its default of 'Normal'. This option causes unconstrained pixels to be assigned a unique color to make them visibly identifiable.

Mu - This impacts the tradeoff between having a dramatic image that is difficult to visualize (larger values) versus a less dramatic image that is easier to visualize (smaller values). The traditional default is 0.333, although a skilled artist can get away with a value as large as 0.5 or even slightly larger. Mathematically, this is the fraction of the distance between the backplane (the furthest distance in the scene) and the viewplane which is traversed as Z ranges from 0 to 1. (The eye is the same distance from the viewplane as the backplane.)   Especially note that hidden pixel problems rapidly proliferate as mu increases, because the closer parts of the object get to the viewplane, the more these parts obscure other parts of the scene.

Attempt fixing hidden pixels - Checking this box tells the program to make educated guesses about the appropriate color to assign to pixels that correspond to hidden parts of the image. More often than not, this provides a significant improvement in scenes that suffer from numerous hidden pixels due to rapid depth changes at large Z values. But occasionally this option makes a real mess of things. If this option is invoked, the 'Interpolate Z when oversampling' option should usually be turned off, as these two options conflict with each other.

Interpolate Z when oversampling - This is meaningful only when 'Oversampling' is set to a value greater than 1. This option causes the depth to be linearly interpolated across each oversample group, rather than taking discrete jumps for each group. Unless the 'Attempt fixing hidden pixels' option has been invoked, this is virtually always highly beneficial. The combination of this option with large oversampling is nearly always capable of eliminating all rapid-depth-change anomalies other than hidden pixel issues. The mechanism by which this works is discussed on Page 72.

Apply 3-column median filter - For each row, each set of three adjacent pixels in the final image is considered. For each color channel (RGB) separately, the median of the three pixels is computed and used for the final image. This usually produces a very small, almost invisible, improvement of image quality by filtering out computational noise.

Apply 3-row median filter - For each column, each set of three adjacent pixels in the final image is considered. For each color channel (RGB) separately, the median of the three pixels is computed and used for the final image. This usually produces a very small, almost invisible, improvement of image quality by filtering out computational noise.

Cuda device usage - This is relevant for only the CUDA version of the program.

Cuda split - This is relevant for only the CUDA version of the program.

Mapped Texture Single Object

A stereogram using the single-object texture mapping method is computed and displayed. A texture image and a depth image must be present. These images must be the same height (number of rows) and width (number of columns). The generated stereogram will have the same dimensions as the texture and depth images.

In nearly all practical applications, this stereogram will not stand alone as a final product. Rather, it will be overlaid onto a sprite-method stereogram that serves as the background, usually (though not necessarily) at the backplane.

Pixels fall into one of two categories: *background* and *object*. A pixel is background if its texture is pure black: R=G=B=0. Otherwise it is object. One implication is that the texture map cannot use pure black as a color for the object. In practice this is no limitation, because setting one of the colors to the minimum nonzero value will make it appear black to any observer. But it is a detail to which one must pay attention, because if some pixels in the object are pure black, things may get messy. Background pixels are ignored, both in the texture image and the depth image.

Single-object texture-mapped stereograms are called 'single-object' because only one of the instances of the object stands out from the backplane, that corresponding to the object pixels in the depth image. All other instances appear as if they are painted onto the backplane. They are generally used in either of two ways:

If the object is narrow enough in each of its rows that no overlap of instances occurs (the object width in each row is well under about 1/3 the eye separation) then we will see a single, well-defined object projecting out from the backplane. No unusual precautions need to be taken in the object's design, although of course the usual warnings about sudden depth changes, especially at large Z values, apply. The object will be a relatively small component of the overall stereogram, at least when individual rows are considered.

The other use is when the object occupies most of the stereogram. In this application, the object is the primary component of the work of art, the focus of the observer. Design of the object is much more critical in this situation, because there will be massive overlap of instances. Thus, it is incumbent on the artist to minimize the the number of of columns in each row that are part of the object. A classic example of this is for the object to be a framework of a larger object, such as a cube constructed of narrow girders. The idea is that any time two object pixels in a row compete for representation in the stereogram, we have a conflict that can confuse the eye. The simplest solution is to minimize the number of object pixels in each row, which in turn minimizes the potential for conflicts, although careful (and difficult!) design of the object can shift parts of the object in such a way that conflicts are minimized.

The other consideration for this second use, dominance of the object in the stereogram, is that the object should be such that the human eye and brain can instinctively 'fix' observed conflicts without being overly aware of them. For example, a skeleton of a well-known object can easily have any gaps 'filled in' by a viewer who recognizes the object. On the other hand, something like a face will painfully reveal any flaws. The bottom line is that this second use can require careful design and usually a lot of trial and error.

The following information must be supplied by the user:

Eye spacing - This is the number of columns separating the viewer's eyes. If this stereogram is overlaid onto a sprite-based stereogram, the usual situation, it is critical that *the eye separation used here be the same as the eye separation used for the sprite-based background*. Failure to do so will results in all sorts of unpleasant anomalies when the overlay is performed. See the prior section on sprite-based stereograms for more details on this parameter.

Oversampling rate - For rapid experimentation and confirmation of quality, this should be left at its default of 1. If it is set to a value greater than 1, each row is stretched out into the original number of columns times this quantity. Computations are done on this extended row, and then the final stereogram is computed by averaging the tones in each oversample group. This is extremely beneficial, as it reduces or even eliminates (if oversampling is large enough) anomalies due to rapid depth changes. The need for oversampling depends on the presence of sudden large changes in depth.

Mu - This impacts the tradeoff between having a dramatic image that is difficult to visualize (larger values) versus a less dramatic image that is easier to visualize (smaller values). If this stereogram is overlaid onto a sprite-based stereogram, the usual situation, it is critical that *the mu used here be the same as the mu used for the sprite-based background*. Failure to do so will result in all sorts of unpleasant anomalies when the overlay is performed. See the prior section on sprite-based stereograms for more details on this parameter.

Attempt fixing hidden pixels - Checking this box tells the program to make educated guesses about the appropriate color to assign to pixels that correspond to hidden parts of the image. More often than not, this provides a significant improvement in scenes that suffer from numerous hidden pixels due to rapid depth changes at large Z values. But occasionally this option makes a real mess of things. If this option is invoked, the 'Interpolate Z when oversampling' option should usually be turned off, as these two options conflict with each other.

Interpolate Z when oversampling - This is meaningful only when 'Oversampling' is set to a value greater than 1. This option causes the depth to be linearly interpolated across each oversample group, rather than taking discrete jumps for each group. Unless the 'Attempt fixing hidden pixels' option has been invoked, this is virtually always highly beneficial. The combination of this option with large oversampling is nearly always capable of eliminating all rapid-depth-change anomalies other than hidden pixel issues. The mechanism by which this works is discussed on Page 72.

Apply 3-column median filter - For each row, each set of three adjacent pixels in the final image is considered. For each color channel (RGB) separately, the median of the three pixels is computed and used for the final image. This usually produces a very small, almost invisible, improvement of image quality by filtering out computational noise.

Apply 3-row median filter - For each column, each set of three adjacent pixels in the final image is considered. For each color channel (RGB) separately, the median of the three pixels is computed and used for the final image. This usually produces a very small, almost invisible, improvement of image quality by filtering out computational noise.

Favor Z versus averaging overlap - Most commonly, the texture object will be narrow enough (well under about 1/3 of the eye separation) that overlap of instances does not occur. However, some specialized applications such as the example given on Page 92 deliberately use an object so wide that overlap occurs. By default, when multiple instances compete to determine the color of a viewplane pixel, their average is used for the stereogram pixel. Checking this box causes the object pixel closest to the viewplane (maximum Z) to be used instead. Usually, averaging is better, but in some (rare!) cases, using the maximum Z is better.

Trim left partial instance - It often happens that an instance of the object gets partially cut off at the left edge of the stereogram, resulting in a partial representation of the instance. Some artists may find this ugly, and others may not. Checking this box causes partial instances at the left edge to be completely removed. This is a purely artistic decision, as long as at least 4 instances are visible. For this to work properly, it must be possible to draw a vertical line to the right of the leftmost instance, with this line completely to the left of the next instance.

Trim right partial instance - This is identical to the prior option, except that it applies to the right edge of the stereogram.

Cuda device usage - This is relevant for only the CUDA version of the program.

Cuda split - This is relevant for only the CUDA version of the program.

Mapped Texture Multiple Object

A stereogram using the multiple-object texture-mapping method is computed and displayed. A texture image and a depth image must be present. These images must be the same height (number of rows) and width (number of columns). The generated stereogram will have the same dimensions as the texture and depth images.

In nearly all practical applications, this stereogram will not stand alone as a final product. Rather, it will be overlaid onto a sprite-method stereogram that serves as the background, usually (though not necessarily) at the backplane.

Pixels fall into one of two categories: *background* and *object*. A pixel is background if its texture is pure black: R=G=B=0. Otherwise it is object. One implication is that the texture map cannot use pure black as a color for the object. In practice this is no limitation, because setting one of the colors to the minimum nonzero value will make it appear black to any observer. But it is a detail to which one must pay attention, because if some pixels in the object are pure black, things may get messy. Background pixels are ignored, both in the texture image and the depth image.

Multiple-object texture-mapped stereograms are called 'multiple-object' because every instance of the object stands out from the backplane. The object *must* be narrow enough in each of its rows that no overlap of instances occurs (the object width in each row is under about 1/3 the eye separation). No unusual precautions need to be taken in the object's design, although of course the usual warnings about sudden depth changes, especially at large Z values, apply. Each instance of the object will be a relatively small component of the overall stereogram but repeated left-to-right.

With 'normal' vision, just looking at the stereogram as a picture, a multiple-object stereogram and a single-object stereogram will appear nearly identical, multiple instances of the object arrayed across the image.

But when one employs '3D' vision, the difference becomes clear. With the single-object version, exactly one of the object instances will pop out of the backplane, while with the multiple-object version, every instance will pop out.

The following information must be supplied by the user:

Eye spacing - This is the number of columns separating the viewer's eyes. If this stereogram is overlaid onto a sprite-based stereogram, the usual situation, it is critical that *the eye separation used here be the same as the eye separation used for the sprite-based background*. Failure to do so will results in all sorts of unpleasant anomalies when the overlay is performed. See the earlier section on sprite-based stereograms for more details on this parameter.

Oversampling rate - For rapid experimentation and confirmation of quality, this should be left at its default of 1. If it is set to a value greater than 1, each row is stretched out into the original number of columns times this quantity. Computations are done on this extended row, and then the final stereogram is computed by averaging the tones in each oversample group. This is extremely beneficial, as it reduces or even eliminates (if oversampling is large enough) anomalies due to rapid depth changes. The need for oversampling depends on the presence of sudden large changes in depth.

Mu - This impacts the tradeoff between having a dramatic image that is difficult to visualize (larger values) versus a less dramatic image that is easier to visualize (smaller values). If this stereogram is overlaid onto a sprite-based stereogram, the usual situation, it is critical that *the mu used here be the same as the mu used for the sprite-based background*. Failure to do so will result in all sorts of unpleasant anomalies when the overlay is performed. See the earlier section on sprite-based stereograms for more details on this parameter.

Attempt fixing hidden pixels - Checking this box tells the program to make educated guesses about the appropriate color to assign to pixels that correspond to hidden parts of the image. More often than not, this provides a significant improvement in scenes that suffer from numerous hidden pixels due to rapid depth changes at large Z values. But occasionally this option makes a real mess of things. If this option is invoked, the 'Interpolate Z when oversampling' option should usually be turned off, as these two options conflict with each other.

Interpolate Z when oversampling - This is meaningful only when 'Oversampling' is set to a value greater than 1. This option causes the depth to be linearly interpolated across each oversample group, rather than taking discrete jumps for each group. Unless the 'Attempt fixing hidden pixels' option has been invoked, this is virtually always highly beneficial. The combination of this option with large oversampling is nearly always capable of eliminating all rapid-depth-change anomalies other than hidden pixel issues. The mechanism by which this works is discussed on Page 72.

Apply 3-column median filter - For each row, each set of three adjacent pixels in the final image is considered. For each color channel (RGB) separately, the median of the three pixels is computed and used for the final image. This usually produces a very small, almost invisible, improvement of image quality by filtering out computational noise.

Apply 3-row median filter - For each column, each set of three adjacent pixels in the final image is considered. For each color channel (RGB) separately, the median of the three pixels is computed and used for the final image. This usually produces a very small, almost invisible, improvement of image quality by filtering out computational noise.

Favor Z versus averaging overlap - This will be irrelevant for multiple-object stereograms in the vast majority of applications. This is because the artist should make sure that, in each row, the object is narrow enough to prevent overlap (under about 1/3 the eye separation). Checking this box causes the object pixel closest to the viewplane (maximum Z) to be used instead of averaging in case of overlap conflict. But we really should not have conflict! Keep the object narrow.

Trim left partial instance - It often happens that an instance of the object gets partially cut off at the left edge of the stereogram, resulting in a partial representation of the instance. Some artists may find this ugly, and others may not. Checking this box causes partial instances at the left edge to be completely removed. This is a purely artistic decision, as long as at least 4 instances are visible. For this to work properly, it must be possible to draw a vertical line to the right of the leftmost instance, with this line completely to the left of the next instance.

Trim right partial instance - This is identical to the prior option, except that it applies to the right edge of the stereogram.

Cuda device usage - This is relevant for only the CUDA version of the program.

Cuda split - This is relevant for only the CUDA version of the program.

Flat Stereo Image

This is a quick-and-easy way to construct a stereogram that will (usually) serve as a background onto which texture-mapped stereograms will be overlaid. This operation is used when you want a stereogram that has constant depth (Z) across its entire extent. Thus, only a sprite image is employed; if a depth image is present, it is ignored.

The user must supply five quantities: the number of rows and columns of the desired stereogram, the eye separation, mu, and the desired Z (0-1, usually 0 to make it a backplane). It is crucial that the eye separation and mu be exactly the same as the quantities that will be used for the texture-mapped stereograms that will be overlaid onto this background.

The dimensions of the sprite image are irrelevant, because the entire sprite will be employed, being rescaled as needed. No vertical tiling or truncation takes place; the full height of the sprite is mapped to the desired height of the stereogram. The full width of the sprite, rescaled as needed, will be tiled in accord with the desired width of the stereogram, the specified mu, and the specified eye separation. If Z=0, each tile will have a width equal to half the eye separation.

Most often, the artist will specify Z=0 and use this stereogram as the background 'canvas' onto which to overlay one or more texture-mapped stereograms. But there are two other clever uses that can be exploited by a skilled artist.

One use is to set Z to a small positive value, perhaps 0.05 to 0.1 to create a transparent or partial secondary background in front of a primary Z=0 background. You could fully color the sprite and overlay it onto the primary background with transparency set to 0.5 or so, creating the effect of a translucent curtain in front of the backplane. Alternatively, you could have most of the sprite be pure black (R=G=B=0), with the rest of it being a pleasing pattern. When this is overlaid onto the primary background, it will create an interesting decorative effect, because black pixels in an overlay are ignored. Most or all objects in the scene would then be given larger Z values, situating them in front of this secondary background.

The other use is to set Z=1 or some other large value. By fully coloring the sprite and doing a transparent overlay as the last step in the artistic creation, you will create the effect of a theatrical scrim curtain, blurring the objects behind it. Or, as in the other use, you could leave most of the sprite pure black, employing a skimpy pattern, and doing a fully opaque overlay. This will give the effect of a decorative 3D frame around and in front of your scene.

It must be emphasized that when Z is 1 or nearly so for a scrim or fancy frame effect, this overlay *must* be the last step. Otherwise, subsequent placement of objects will pierce holes in the curtain, something unlikely to be pretty (although it may be interesting!).

Copy Image-to-Image

One image is copied to another image, with optional expansion by padding with a pure black frame around the source image. This is not resampling; the source image remains at its same size. But if the destination image is specified to be larger than the source image, pure black rows and/or columns are appended to the top, bottom, left, and right as specified by the user.

The user specifies four quantities: the final number of rows and columns, a row offset in percent (0-100), and a similar column offset.

If the number of rows or columns is specified to be zero, the copied image has the same dimension as the source image, and the offsets are ignored. The number of rows/columns cannot be reduced, only kept the same or increased by black padding.

If the number of rows is specified larger than the number of rows in the source, black rows are added above and/or below. The amount above and below is controlled by the row offset. The default of 50 applies equal padding above and below. Deviations from 50 shift the source image by this amount as a percent of the specified (destination) number of rows, subject to there being a row difference large enough to accommodate the desired shift. For example, suppose the user specifies a row offset of 40 percent. Then the source image will be shifted up inside the destination by 10 percent of the number of destination rows. A similar rule applies to column shifting.

This is a workhorse routine, used to expand texture and depth images to the size of the final stereogram without losing resolution. Use this instead of *Adjust Object Size/Position* whenever possible.

Overlay Image-to-Image

A source image is overlaid onto a destination image. These images must be the same size. Pixels that are pure black (R=G=B=0) in the *source* image are ignored and not overlaid. Thus, pixels in the destination image that correspond to pure black pixels in the source image are unchanged.

The user must specify a transparency, which is used to average source and destination pixels, each color band independently. The default of 0 causes a fully opaque overlay, with source pixels fully replacing destination pixels. Using a transparency of 100 would be pointless, resulting in no overlay at all. A transparency of 50 causes source and destination pixels to be averaged, given equal weight. Intermediate values of transparency control the weighting linearly.

Reverse Overlay

A source image is overlaid onto a destination image. These images must be the same size. Pixels that are pure black (R=G=B=0) in the *destination* image are ignored and do not receive an overlay from the source image. Thus, pixels in the destination image that are pure black remain pure black. Only non-black destination pixels receive the overlay from the source image. If a source pixel to act as overlay is pure black (this should be rare), it is overlaid as the darkest possible gray (R=G=B=1). This way, no destination pixel ever changes from non-black to black.

Adjust Object Size/Position

This operation is a simple means for positioning texture-mapped objects when they are overlaid onto a background. It affects the current texture and depth images, which must be the same size if both are present. (It is legal to have just one of them present, but this would be highly unusual. In the vast majority of situations, both texture and its corresponding depth will be present when adjusting.)

If a texture image is present, the usual situation, pixels that are pure black (R=G=B=0) are background, and all other pixels are object. If only a depth image is present, pixels with a depth of 0 are background, and all other pixels are object.

If the *Adjust vertical* box is checked, the object is adjusted vertically. The user specifies the desired top and bottom columns for final placement. The object may be expanded, although this would be unusual. In most cases, the object will have been generated at high resolution and then shrunk for placement in the stereogram. The object's horizontal size and position are similarly adjusted if the 'Adjust horizontal' box is checked.

The range of Z values in the object is adjusted if the *Adjust Z* box is checked. Also, any pixels below the specified *Depth Floor* have their Z raised to the depth floor before any adjustment is done. This is useful if the depth image has one or more very small Z pixels below the apparent, desired bottom of the object.

The backplane Z value (Z of background pixels, almost always 0) is specified via the *Backplane Z* value.

Note that this operation costs image resolution if the size is reduced! Whenever possible, use the *Copy Image-to-Image* option instead, because that operation preserves full resolution.

Split Object at Depth

This option is primarily used to facilitate having an object be split by a transparent overly, such as something partially submerged in water with a transparent surface. The user specifies a Z depth threshold, 0-1, and a checkbox specifying whether we are to keep the upper (Z greater than or equal to threshold) or lower (Z less than threshold) part of the object. Note that if any part of the upper section extends over an area of the lower section, the algorithm is imperfect for the lower section and can sometimes give strange 3D results.

The usual process is as follows, and a detailed example appears on Page 76.
　　　1) If the upper part never extends over the lower part, create a stereo image from the bottom part. Otherwise create the stereo image from the entire object.
　　　2) Overlay a transparent stereo layer onto that stereo image, with the depth of the overlay equal to the splitting depth.
　　　3) Create a stereo image of the top part and overlay that fully opaque.

If we were to not use this approach, and instead overlay the entire object in Step 3, any parts of the object that are outside the part above the transparent overlay and have depth below the transparent overlay would destructively pierce the transparent overlay and make it vanish there.

Depth Red from Texture

This is one of two ways to assign the red channel in a 24-bit depth file to important columns. For each row, the first and last columns of the object in that row are found. (An object pixel is defined as a pixel in the texture file which is not pure black.) The red channel is set for the mean column ((first+last)/2), thus distributing importance equally on both sides of the center. The texture and depth images must have the same dimensions.

Work1 Red to Depth

This is one of two ways to assign the red channel in a 24-bit depth file to important columns. The red channel in the Work1 image is copied to the depth image. The usual way this would be used is to make a copy of the texture image and modify its colors as needed to make sure the red channel is less than 128 everywhere. Then manually draw red (red tone at least 128) as needed through the texture to mark the importance for each row. The dimensions of Work1 and Depth must be identical. For sprite-based stereograms the red would be a line marking the center of importance, while super-texture for single-object texture-based stereograms requires the focus area to be completely blocked out in red.

Mask Depth from Texture

Every pixel in the depth file that does not have a non-pure-black corresponding texture pixel is set to zero. This is useful for making texture-mapped stereograms when it is difficult to make a depth map along with the texture map. You can just create a simple full-image depth map that has the general characteristics desired, perhaps by using a function-generated depth map. Then use this option to mask out all depth pixels that do not correspond to the object. The texture and depth images must have the same dimensions.

Resample Sprite

The sprite image is resampled to make it larger or smaller. No smoothing, interpolating, or antialiasing is done, so this is a pretty crude operation. If you need quality resampling, you should use a professional image editor.

Smooth Depth

A simple moving-average block filter is applied to the depth image. Only pixels that are not zero depth (B=G=0) are adjusted; all zero-depth pixels remain zero depth. Only non-zero-depth pixels go into computation of the average for the filtered value. This prevents the depth of valid texture pixels from being pulled down by zero-depth pixels just outside the texture area.

Note that this total ignoring of zero-depth pixels implies that there is a one-to-one correspondence between non-zero depth pixels and texture pixels. Non-texture pixels should have zero depth, and texture pixels should have nonzero depth. The first requirement is easily satisfied by the *Mask depth from texture* option if it did not automatically happen when the depth image was generated. The second requirement is easily satisfied by the *Adjust object size/position* option if the original depth image has any zero-depth pixels within the texture (a very unusual situation).

This operation, especially across columns, is usually an effective way to remove black speckling on texture-based stereograms. Imagine that you are looking down at a staircase, directly above it, and then you move back slightly. The front edge of each stair will hide the back edge of the stair below. This hiding can cause hidden-pixel speckling in a stereogram, especially a texture-based version, in which case the hidden pixels appear as tiny black dots or even thick black lines. If the stairs are differing heights (different rates of depth change across the depth image), taller stairs (more rapid depth change) will cause more hiding. Depth smoothing evens out the rate of depth change and will often cause a profound improvement in the appearance of the stereogram.

3

Essential Stereogram Techniques

Sprite-Based Stereograms

This and the next few sections contain simple, educational, but not necessarily pretty demonstrations of the four types of stereogram available in the *Stereo* program. These demonstrations serve as building blocks from which more complex projects can be constructed.

Background from a Flat Stereogram

The first step in implementing any project is to decide on the final stereogram dimensions and the number of background repetitions (dependent on FAR as defined on Page 103). Larger images take more time to compute, but this is rarely a problem with modern computers. The most important consideration concerning size is print resolution. We want at least 300 DPI (dots per inch) for good results. For this project, I want a width of 7 inches, so using 2400 columns provides 343 DPI. Using a height of 1800 pixels provides a roughly 'Golden Ratio' size with square pixels.

The number of background repetitions can be as small as 4 in some specialized applications, but using more repetitions provides easier visualization, especially for beginners. On the other hand, using too many produces a cluttered image in most cases. So 5 to 6 repetitions (it need not be an integer) is common. I chose 6 for this example and many stereogram demonstrations in this book. Thus, we need the background sprite to have 2400/6=400 columns. My chosen sprite is shown in Figure 4.

This sprite is used to create a background for the various simple ring demonstrations that follow. One could use an image editor to tile six of them side-by-side, but an easier way is to use the *Flat Stereo Image* option to create the background image. We fill in the number of rows (1800) and columns (2400). This is a background image, so specify Z=0. We stick with the default mu=0.3333. Finally, recall that for Z=0 the eye separation will be twice the repetition width; 400 * 2 = 800. This produces the background image shown on the next page in Figure 5.

Figure 4

Figure 5: Full background image for ring demonstrations

Primitive Sprite Stereogram

We'll set that full background aside for a moment to demonstrate a 'traditional' primitive sprite-based stereogram. We'll use Figure 4 as the background sprite, and use the depth map shown in Figure 6 (displayed smaller than its full 7" width). Because for this type of stereogram we do not have to correlate with a precomputed background image, which we will need to do later, we have some latitude in choosing the eye separation, though it still should be very close to double the sprite width. It turns out that when using 800, which we used a moment ago for the background, a couple of minor but annoying glitches appeared. This often happens when the depth has large, sudden changes, which is certainly the case here. The ring stands out far in front of the backplane, with the depth gapping between 0 and values as large as its maximum of 0.7 in a single column, with no smooth connection. This problematic situation is often remedied by fiddling with the eye spacing a little. Here, using a spacing of 760 instead of 800 completely solves the problem, as shown in Figure 7 on the next page.

Why is the ring bluish instead of white? Recall (and we'll see later many times) that the red channel in the depth image has special uses, so it's a good idea to use an external image editing program to zero it out.

Figure 6: Ring depth map for sprite stereogram

Figure 7: Primitive sprite-based stereogram

Texture on a Sprite-Based Stereogram

With considerable care, it is possible to impose a small texture onto a sprite-based stereogram. This is useful when you want the majority of the object to be hidden from ordinary vision, as is the case for sprite-based stereograms, but you want to highlight some small but important part of the object. One classic example is when your object is a person or animal which you want mostly hidden, but you want it to have a clearly defined face. Here, we will modify the ring example just seen by isolating the diamond (with an external image editor), reading it into the *Texture* window, and overlaying it onto the Figure 5 background (the sprite image), as shown in Figure 8. (This is not a stereogram yet! Please keep reading.)

Figure 8: Diamond overlaid onto background

We also use the *Depth Red from Texture* operation to define the depth image's red channel to be the center of the diamond for each row, as shown in Figure 9. We had to moderately shrink the ring in the background and depth images before doing these things, because the diamond is wider than half the eye separation, and we must ensure that there is no overlap of the diamond instances on the stereogram. If any instances overlap, the 3D effect usually will not suffer, but the appearance of the texture will be damaged, often severely.

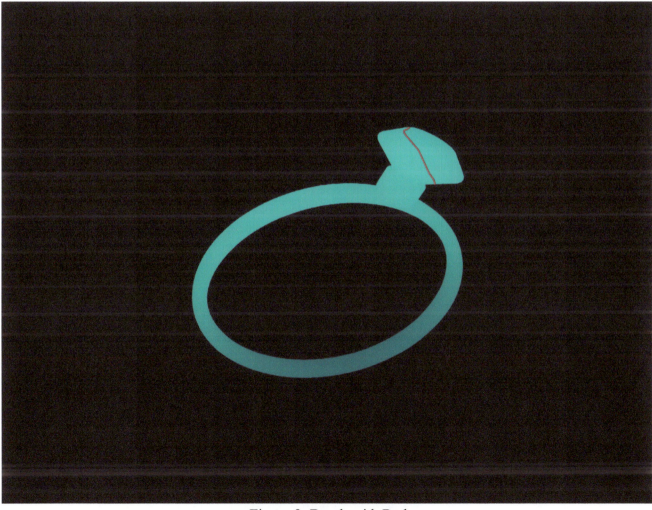

Figure 9: Depth with Red

The resulting stereogram is shown in Figure 10. The eye separation had to be 800 so as to match the eye separation used to create the background. Note that the diamond must be positioned on the background so as to perfectly correspond with the position of the diamond in the depth map. This is easily done with any good image editing program.

Figure 10: Sprite-based stereogram with diamond texture from overlay

Texture-Mapped Stereograms

The real breakthrough in stereogram generation came with the realization that, subject to some restrictions, a stereogram could be made without use of a background sprite, and an actual image (called a *texture*) could be the entire basis for the stereogram. With this approach, the object would no longer be entirely hidden, as is the case with a sprite-based stereogram. However, the increase in realism and beauty often makes the loss of the 'wow' hidden-object effect worthwhile. And of course, a skilled artist can combine the two types of stereogram by thoughtful overlay and produce some incredible effects. This section explores the two most common uses for texture-mapped stereograms, ultimately demonstrating them both in a single image.

A texture-mapped stereogram in *Stereo* comes in two versions: single-object and multiple-object. A single object is supplied for both methods; the difference between 'single' and 'multiple' refers to final appearance, not the number of objects supplied. They both require that the user provide a texture file and a depth file having the same dimensions and with the position of the object being identical in both images. A pixel is said to be part of the object if its color in the texture file is anything but pure black (R=G=B=0).

For each row (considered individually), the total width of the object must be comfortably less than about 1/3 of the eye separation so that no overlap of instances occur. (There are several arguable exceptions to this rule that will be considered later.) If the object is too wide, resulting in overlap, the appearance of the texture image will be impacted, usually badly. Note, though, that because each row is considered separately, the actual object can span much of the entire width of the scene; it just has to shift horizontally so that there is no overlap in any single row.

To produce this demonstration, the ring texture and depth images were adjusted with the *Adjust object size/position* option. The ring was shrunk to a width of 350 pixels and a height of 260 pixels, with Z ranging from 0.3 to 0.7. A lot of resolution is lost with this approach, and later we will see a more complex alternative method (*Copy Image to Image*) that preserves full resolution. But this is fast and easy. This shrinking was done twice, producing one pair of texture/depth files in which the ring is raised above the center of the image, and another pair with the ring placed well below center. In both cases the ring is kept centered. With texture-mapped stereograms, the object can be shifted away from center, but if it gets too close to the edge bad things happen. So it's safest to keep the object as centered as possible unless the design requires off-center positioning.

The single-object version with an eye separation of 800 was generated using the upper-positioned ring. (This exact separation is required because we will soon overlay the stereograms on the background that was also generated with 800.) The resulting stereogram is shown in Figure 11. You should be able to visualize the depth even without the presence of a background. Note that only one ring appears in front of the backplane; other images are just background instances. The position of the object in the texture and depth maps determines the position of the visualized object.

Figure 11: Single-object stereogram

The multiple-object version was generated using the lower-positioned ring. The resulting stereogram is shown in Figure 12. Multiple rings appear in front of the backplane; the position of the object in the texture and depth maps determines left/right shifting of the visualized objects. The partial instance at the left and right sides are common for both types of stereogram. They cause no problems with visualization, but if the artist finds them ugly they can safely be removed with an external image editor. The automatic removal options in *Stereo* require a bit more separation in order to work correctly.

Figure 12: Multiple-object stereogram

Finally, these two stereograms are overlaid onto the Figure 5 background using the *overlay image-to-image* tool. Use of a pretty background almost always makes for a nicer image, and it also aids in achieving 3D vision because it provides a well defined backplane that acts as a powerful cue to the brain when the eyes are adjusted correctly. This final image is shown in Figure 13.

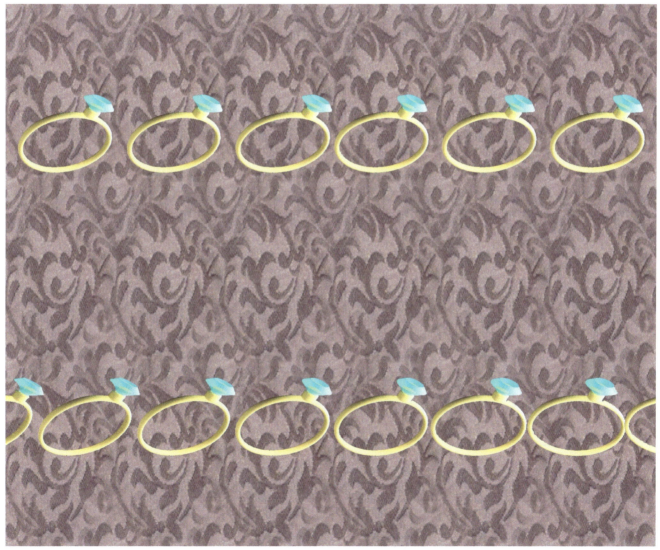

Figure 13: Both stereograms overlaid onto background

An Exception to the Overlap Rule

It has been emphasized that in order to avoid damage to the texture image of the object, the width of the object in each row should be under about 1/3 the eye spacing so as to avoid overlap. Even small overlap usually does severe damage to the object's appearance. But a notable exception to this rule is when any overlapping parts of the object are minimal, perhaps a framework or a thin ring (!). In this case, overlap errors are minimal and may often be acceptable. If there are few object pixels in a row, there are few opportunities for error in that row. Figure 14 shows a single-object texture-mapped stereogram of the ring using our standard 800-pixel eye spacing. The maximum object width is 984 pixels, far from being well under 800/3=267! There is enormous overlap of the gold ring, yet many artists would find the distortion an acceptable tradeoff for having a very wide texture map.

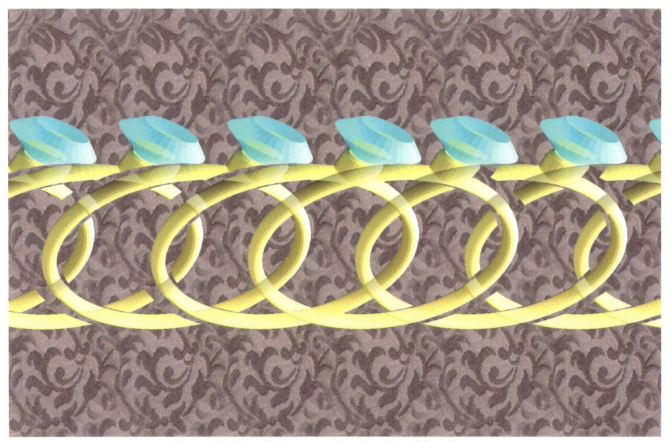

Figure 14: Overlap can work when the object is sparse

Another Exception to the Overlap Rule

We just saw that it can be possible for instances to (mostly) harmlessly overlap if the object occupies little area. The other situation in which overlap distortion may be tolerable is if the object has a nondescript texture pattern, as opposed to being highly recognizable (a face, for example). For this, I created a crude Fire Raptor, as shown in Figure 15. (Yeah, my artistic talent is abysmal). It could be shrunk using the *Adjust Object Size/Position* option, but I wanted to preserve all possible texture, so instead I used the *Copy Image-to-Image* option with the *New Cols* parameter set to four times the original value, and *New Rows* slightly increased. This pads the image with a black background, fully preserving resolution of the object.

Since I drew this object freehand, I did not have an automatically generated depth image. I wanted the bird to be tilted so as to give the appearance of looking up at it in the sky, so a simple way to do this was to use the following simple function to create a rectangular depth map the same size as the padded texture image:

```
Z = (5 - 2 * X - 3 * (1-Y)) / 5 ;
```

As X ranges from 0 (left side) to 1 (right side), Z decreases, and as Y ranges from 0 (bottom) to 1 (top), Z increases. Z has its maximum of 1 at the upper-left corner, and its minimum of 0 at the lower-right corner.

In order to massage this rectangular depth map into one that corresponds to the texture, I used the *Mask Depth from Texture* option, followed by *Adjust Object Size/Position* to expand the range of Z to 0.3-0.8 without needlessly changing the position of the object. Note that this approach results in fewer depth values than ideal, since the range of the function depth map over the extent of the texture is just a fraction of the 0-255 possible. Ideally, the depth map function would have been more sophisticated, covering most or all of the 0-255 range in its central region where the object resides. But I kept it simple for this demonstration. The degradation is so slight as to be almost invisible.

The single-object texture-mapped stereogram is shown in Figure 16. I used an image editor to remove some of the top and bottom rows, which are just cloud background. Since the object resides in the center of the image, I decided to feature it with this selective cropping. Note that the tail of one instance overlaps the wing of the instance to its left. This produces enormous disruption in the texture mapping, obliterating the wing on the left side of the image and removing much of the tail on the right side. (This is called occlusion and is discussed in detail later.) But the errors are almost completely invisible using 3D vision due to the fact that the texture is just a cluttered pattern rather than something easily recognizable.

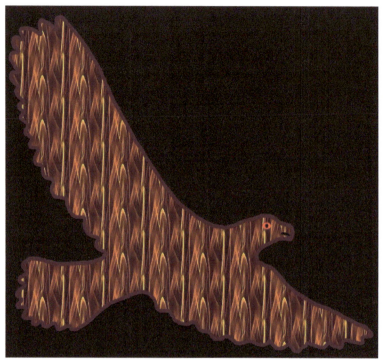

Figure 15: Fire Raptor texture object

Figure 16: Overlap can work when the object has no recognizable pattern

Preserving Overlapped Focus With Overlays

In the prior section we saw that we could often get away with overlap in a single-object stereogram as long as the texture of the object is a simple repetitive pattern rather than a complex, recognizable pattern like a face. The texture is still severely distorted by the overlap, but we probably will not see, or at least be bothered by, distortion in a simple repetitive pattern such as that used for the fire raptor.

But what if there is some relatively small part of the texture that *is* important and that we do not want distorted? There are primarily two techniques that can often protect the integrity of a critical portion of the texture despite massive overlap distortion elsewhere. The *overlay* method will be discussed in this section, and the *super-texture* method presented in the next section.

Consider Figure 17, which shows a large rock with a glowing crystal perched on a natural overhang. We want to create a stereogram of this image, and feature the rock prominently, occupying the majority of the image. But because the rock is so wide, major distortion-inducing overlap is inevitable. The texture pattern of the rock is simple and distributed throughout the rock. Unfortunately, intermingling of the purple crystal and the grey rock will be beyond ugly, totally destroying the effect we want, if we approach the problem naively. We now show a way to keep the crystal intact amid the chaos of the rock distortion.

Figure 17: Rock and crystal for stereogram

The method used here is to create separate stereograms of the rock and the crystal. We then overlay the more important object, the crystal, on top of the less important object, the rock. The tricky part is aligning them correctly. The *Adjust object size/position* option handles this well, but the process can still involve a lot of trial and error. The best procedure is to use the *Copy image-to-image* option to expand both object images to the full size of the stereogram, placing the object that will be moved, the crystal here, in the *Texture* slot, and placing the rock in a working slot. Adjust the position of the crystal to what looks about right (a ruler on the screen helps a lot) and then overlay it onto the rock to see if it is correct. If it's not perfect, reload the rock and adjust again, repeating until you've got it perfect. Write down the final row and column coordinates.

That's only half of the adjustment battle. The crystal's depth dimension remains, but finalizing that adjustment has to wait. Adjust the depth range of the rock as desired (I used 0.2 to 0.7 for this demonstration), create its stereogram (Figure 18), and save that stereogram to a work area and optionally to disk. Then make a good guess for the depth range of the crystal (I used 0.62 to 0.67 here), create its stereogram (Figure 19), and save that stereogram to a work area and optionally to disk. Overlay the crystal's stereogram onto the rock's stereogram and examine it carefully with 3D vision so that you can correct your initial guess for the crystal's depth range. Repeat creation and overlay of the crystal's stereogram until its depth range is perfect. After all positions are finalized, I like to perform the operations one more time to avoid any distortions induced by multiple repositioning.

The final result, overlaid onto a starry background, is shown in Figure 20.

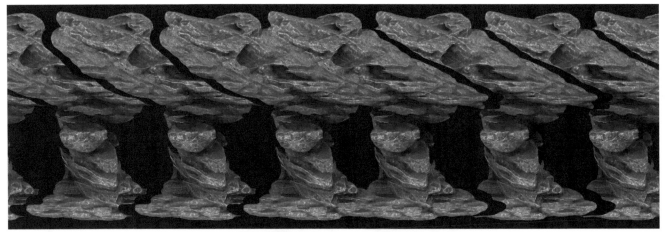

Figure 18: Rock-only single-object stereogram

Note two things about Figure 20. First, the crystal destructively impinges onto the rock on the bottom of the leftward overhang. This is often unavoidable, though with careful planning it can be minimized. Remember that our goal here is to keep the crystal intact, and we fully succeeded. Second, observe that the rock is placed on a lava-streaked 'floor' that approaches the viewer. This is a very advanced process that will be discussed on Page 83.

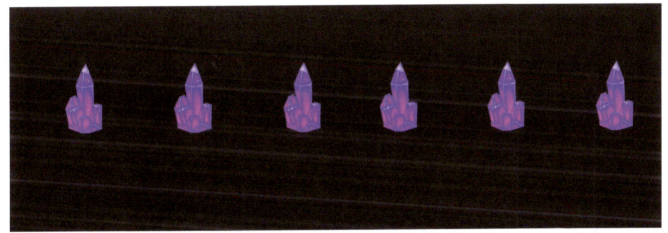

Figure 19: Crystal-only stereogram

Figure 20: Final stereogram

Preserving Overlapped Focus With Super-Texture

The technique described in this section is not often used, because in those situations in which it *can* be used it is often not necessary; focus is already well preserved. In many cases, the area for which texture must be preserved is already isolated enough from the rest of the texture that it is automatically preserved. For example, the texture may be a person whose face is to be preserved, but the face has relatively narrow width and is at the top of the image. Thus, no row of the face will be overlapped, and so the face will be preserved automatically.

However, it occasionally happens that the area to be preserved does have significant overlap with other parts of the complete texture, and this area is an intrinsic part of the object. In the prior example with a rock and crystal, the rock and the crystal are independent objects, so they can be processed separately and then overlaid. But what if we are dealing with a face? It would be extremely difficult, if not impossible, to separate the face from the object, process them separately, and then recombine them. In such situations, the method of *super-texture* can be a lifesaver.

An ideal way to demonstrate this technique is to employ a creature whose face is horizontally aligned with the rest of its body, so that when overlap occurs the face will be conflated with the body. The fish shown in Figure 21 fits the bill nicely.

Figure 21: Fish for super-texture demonstration

On Page 42, when we discussed texture preservation for sprite-based stereograms, we saw (in Figure 9) that we need to draw a red line on the depth image to define the center of the area of interest. For imposing super-texture on a single-object texture-mapped stereogram the procedure is slightly different. Instead of drawing a single line defining a single pixel for each row, we must block out in red the entire area to be preserved. It is important that the marked area not be so wide that it overlaps for any row, or that row will lose focus definition. The easiest way to do the marking is usually to make a copy of the complete texture image, transform it in such a way that all red is eliminated from it, and then manually paint the area of interest. This is shown in Figure 22.

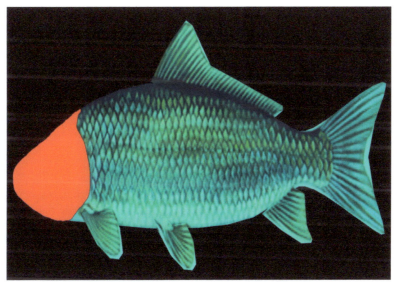

Figure 22: Fish with super-texture painted in red

We would then use the *Copy image-to-image* command to expand it to the full stereogram size, place it in *Work1*, and invoke the *Work1 red to depth* command.

Figure 23 shows the resulting stereogram, with a few bells and whistles thrown in. Note that the face area is completely undistorted, while the 3D effect is maintained perfectly. Of course, the face also appears on the tail, but this is an unavoidable consequence of making the texture so large that it overlaps. The essential point is that without designating the face as super-texture, the face and tail would have blurred together, causing an ugly hybrid to appear in both the face and tail positions. By using super-texture we dictate that the pattern, which *must* appear in both positions to get the correct stereo effect, is the face rather than a hybrid face/tail. And if we hate a face on a tail, we must shrink the fish a little so that there is no overlap!

To produce this stereogram, I created a watery blue background sprite and then stitched a narrow water surface onto the top and a muddy lake bottom onto the bottom of the sprite. The *Make depth backplane* command let me create a depth image suitable for a lake surface and bottom, an advanced technique discussed on Page 83. A simple stereogram based on this sprite provided the complete background.

Then I created a single-object stereogram of the fish and overlaid it onto the stereo background. As a final touch, I created a multiple-object stereogram of a small plant and overlaid it.

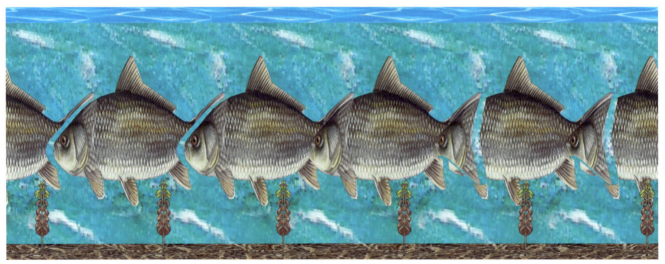

Figure 23: Super-texture demonstration of face preservation

Smoothing to Reduce Hidden-Pixel Problems

The most serious problem that plagues stereogram artists is the impact of hidden pixels. In order for a pixel in the original scene to be visible in correct 3D perspective, it must be visible to both eyes simultaneously. If another part of the image lies between the pixel and either eye, the pair of associated pixels on the stereogram are undefined. This is not a hindrance to 3D vision, because the human brain will instinctively know from context that the hidden pixel is hidden, and not be troubled.

As for ordinary visual appearance (what the stereogram looks like without stereo vision), in a sprite-based stereogram this is usually not a significant issue because the algorithm can just fill in some other part of the background sprite. Since the ordinary-vision appearance of the stereogram is just a mishmash of sprite patterns, this substitution will almost always go unnoticed.

The real problem arises for single-object texture-mapped stereograms. The 'solution' I employ in the *Stereo* program is to color all undefined stereogram pixels as black. This produces an incredibly ugly ordinary-vision display, with any occluding parts of the texture surround by black swaths. But I believe this is still the best approach in that black pixels do not overlay. This gives the artist the opportunity to create a custom background onto which the stereogram can be overlaid and which will hopefully minimize the ordinary-vision impact of the occlusion. We'll see an example of this in the next section. But in this section we consider the possibility that occlusion cannot be tolerated, and we need to prevent it from happening.

A brute-force but usually effective method to reduce or prevent hidden-pixel problems is judicious smoothing of the depth image. If depth changes slowly enough, no occlusion will occur. Of course, in some situations smoothing would introduce intolerable distortion of the shape of the object. When this is the case, you need to either overlay the stereogram on a suitable background, or try a different pose of the object. In most situations, surprisingly little smoothing is needed to solve the problem.

The swimming mermaid shown in Figure 24 presents a particularly difficult example of occlusion. Her right arm is between the observer and her body. I won't bother showing a stereogram done without smoothing; trust me, it's horrendous. Her right arm is surrounded on both sides by strips of black where her body should be. What makes this example difficult is that when we smooth the depth, her arm becomes 'attached' to her body by a ramp. On the other hand, in situations like this when the object is wide, the instances of the object on the stereogram are relatively small, preventing the observer from being aware of this ramping. And it does completely solve the hidden-pixels problem.

Figure 24: Mermaid for demonstrating depth smoothing to prevent occlusion

To produce a single-object texture-mapped stereogram of this mermaid, I expanded the original number of columns, 2400, to 12,000 using the *Copy image-to-image* command. The depth ranged from Z=0.2 to 0.6, and I smoothed it with a vertical half-width of 2 rows and a horizontal half-width of 60 columns. Compared to the 12,000 columns, this is minimal smoothing, yet it is sufficient to completely eliminate occlusion. An eye separation of 4400 packed the instances as close as possible (look at the center of the image) with no actual overlap. Note that by elevating the head and dropping the tail I was able to avoid overlap in any row while still letting the bounding boxes overlap. This is a useful trick for maximizing the size of the object in the stereogram. I overlaid the mermaid stereogram onto a watery background and green ocean bottom (details on Page 83), and finally I added a jewel at Z=0.5, aligned with her hand as if grasping it. The result is shown in Figure 25. Note that when the primary object is wide compared to its height, the resulting stereogram is, of necessity, small due to needing five or so replications across the page. Always keep this in mind when designing a project.

Figure 25: Judicious depth smoothing prevents occlusion by her right arm

Distracting the Observer From Occlusion Problems

If you insist on making the object so large that instances overlap, then occlusion becomes a vastly more serious problem. This is because the primary object that is in front of the backplane will occlude the secondary instances that all lie on the backplane, and this occlusion propagates left and right across the entire stereogram. Moreover, smoothing won't do a thing to help. This is a fundamental mathematical problem, not solvable by any means that I know We saw this in Figure 23, where some parts of the fish occluded other overlapping parts. We also saw it in Figure 18 where overlapping parts of the rock caused occlusion, and in Figure 16 where parts of the Fire Raptor overlapped. Earlier, I just called it 'overlap distortion' or some such thing, but pixel-hiding occlusion is the root of the problem.

In those earlier examples, I approached the problem from the direction of the texture pattern being damaged, and I presented two exceptions to the rule that overlap should be avoided: the object was sparse, as in the ring example, and the texture pattern was not a recognizable object, as shown in the Fire Raptor example. Now I look at exactly the same problem but from a different direction: what do we do about the unavoidably missing occluded parts of the object.

But before venturing further into this topic, I must emphasize one vital point: ***the occlusion problem is a problem of the artist's own making, and it can be completely avoided by preventing overlap.*** I would not want to leave the reader with the idea that the ugliness of occlusion is an omnipresent issue that we must learn to deal with or accept. It is not. It happens *only* when the artist chooses to make the object so wide that instances overlap. And even then, by careful design, we can often have the instance's bounding boxes overlap a lot while still avoiding overlap in a row. Look back at the mermaid stereogram, Figure 25. Do you see how, in the center of the image, the head and tail strongly overlap? Yet there is no occlusion because the head is high and the tail is low; no individual row overlaps, even though the instances strongly overlap in terms of their bounding boxes.

If your object just has to be wide, there are several approaches to consider in order to eliminate or minimize the problem of occlusion:

- Can you make the left side of the object go in where the right side goes out, or go out where the right side goes in? If so, instances can pack more tightly and hence be larger without overlap. Suppose your object is the shape of a *less than* sign, <. You could pack those tightly without occlusion.

- Although smoothing won't do a thing about occlusion due to overlap, it can be almost miraculous at remedying occlusion of one part of the object by another part. If you see black bands to the left and right of a near part of the object, smoothing should be your first line of attack. Always start out small and use as little as possible. Usually, using a half-width of just 1 or 2 rows is optimal, with the vast majority of the smoothing taking place across columns.

- Gaps in the texture map due to occlusion are most prominent when the background that shows through is in stark contrast to the object's texture. This is at its worst when the background is a solid color. The example given in this section demonstrates how to avoid a solid color showing through by careful alignment of object and background.

- The most effective way to hide occlusion gaps is to use a background that closely resembles the object's texture. The next section demonstrates this difficult but highly effective technique.

For now, let's examine the second-to-last point above, aligning the object and the background so that solid colors do not show through occlusion gaps. Just to be clear, ***this demonstration is as much an example of what not to do as what to do***. Superficially, the purpose of this demonstration would seem to be to present a relatively easy method for (hopefully) minimizing the awful visual effect of occlusion due to overlap of object instances. In a way this is the case. But on a deeper level, the more important lesson to be gained from this demonstration is that *preventing the problem while still in the design phase is vastly better than trying to fix it later*. In many cases, the object does not have to be much smaller than you really want in order to avoid overlap. And even when this is not the case, careful planning of the object's pose may allow you to overlap instances significantly while still preventing overlap in any individual row. This is just a matter of having one side of the object be concave when the other side is convex, or having one side be high when the other side is low. In my opinion, if overlap occlusion is unavoidable it might be better to dump the idea and go on to a different project, rather than plugging ahead and then trying to fix occlusion gaps.

For this demonstration we will call on our lovely mermaid again, but this time in a pose that's guaranteed to be problematic. Look at Figure 26 and think about her right arm. When instances of this figure overlap, that arm will cross in front of her neighbor's body, occluding it badly. Also, her wide tail will overlap across instances. A change as simple as rotating her moderately about the vertical axis and bringing her right arm a little closer to her body would fix the problem. But we will assume that the artist is adamant about this pose and would rather fix occlusion problems instead of making small modifications to prevent the problems.

Figure 26: A terrible pose for overlap

Figure 27: Sprite for demo

The background sprite designed for this example, Figure 27, demonstrates two things. The rock will be aligned with the mermaid in such a way that it lies behind the arm/body occlusion rather than having sky or some solid color behind the occlusion. This will give the eye something more complex than just a solid color to look at, and hopefully the observer will be less aware of the ugly occlusion gap. The water below will do just the opposite. It's not a solid color, but it does have relatively little texture. This will make the occlusion gaps in the tail quite visible. Thus, we can demonstrate the difference between a complex, interesting backdrop versus a simpler backdrop, when used for 'hiding' occlusion gaps.

The result is shown in Figure 28. You can decide for yourself how well the kludge of backing up her arm occlusion with a rock works. Personally, I would rather do whatever is needed to avoid occlusion.

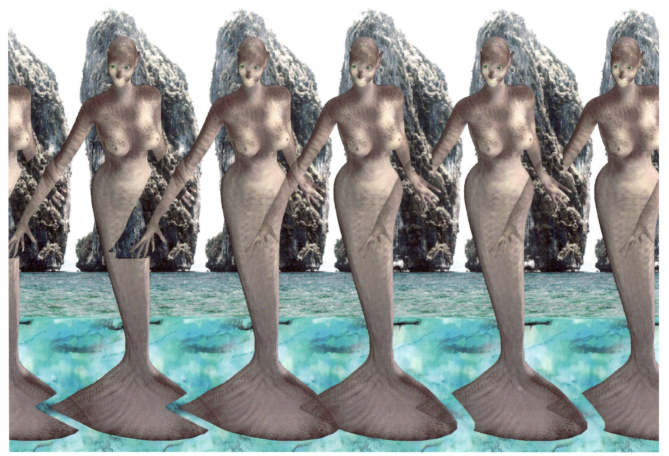

Figure 28: Final stereogram

Camouflaging Occlusion Problems

This section describes a somewhat advanced technique that can be wonderful in the hands of a skilled artist. Suppose you insist on having an object that is so wide that overlap is inevitable, and you are unable to shape or pose it in a way that avoids overlap on all rows. An excellent, though often difficult approach is to use textures and colors that are similar in both the object and the background. The trick is to make the object texture/color close enough to the background texture/color that occluded areas are unobvious while the object itself is well defined. A truly skilled artist can make them so close that the object is almost invisible in normal vision, but jumps out at the viewer in 3D vision.

In Figure 29 I adjusted the colors of the background rock and the Trex to roughly match, and then I reduced the saturation to levels so low that they became almost black-and-white images. This is a low-skill approach to color/texture matching, but it does the trick. It takes careful study in normal vision to see how, on the left, the tail obscures the neighbor's leg, and on the right, the leg and left hand obscure the neighbor's tail. Note that inexperienced observers will find 3D vision difficult to obtain in this example because there are only four instances, while five or six are needed for easy 3D vision. A multiple-object fern in the foreground adds a splotch of needed color.

Figure 29: Camouflaging occlusion

Extreme Camouflage With Reverse Overlays

This section takes the technique of the prior section further, making the color/texture of the object and the background so similar that not only do overlap occlusions become essentially invisible, but the object can be made to blend so intimately into the background that it almost disappears, much as in a sprite-based stereogram. This can be a powerful technique, because aside from solving occlusion problems, it provides a hybrid best-of-both-worlds approach to stereogram creation. With normal vision the object is difficult, if not impossible to discern, but with 3D vision not only does it pop out at the observer, but it has a color/texture that is noticeably different from that of the background, making the object much more prominent than it would be with a sprite-based stereogram.

The key operation for this technique is the *reverse overlay*. The user specifies a destination image, which is usually the object that would otherwise be used as the texture file. A source image is also specified, which typically is similar or identical to the background. Pixels in the source image are substituted for the corresponding pixels in the destination for all destination pixels that are not pure black. Thus, after this operation, the destination has exactly the same division into black and non-black pixels, but the original texture has been replaced by the source texture. To see an example of this, look at the dragon in Figure 30 and the ivy-covered wall in Figure 31. A reverse overlay generates the image in Figure 32.

Figure 30: Dragon texture   Figure 31: Ivy for rev overlay   Figure 32: After rev overlay

If one were to use the image in Figure 32 as a texture image for a single-object texture-mapped stereogram, provide a suitable depth map, and overlay the result onto a flat stereogram of the ivy sprite, one would obtain a result that strongly resembles a sprite-based stereogram. This is shown in Figure 33. But please understand that although there are similarities, there are also differences:

- A texture-mapped stereogram using the background as texture mostly or entirely hides the object in normal vision, just like a sprite-based stereogram.

- For proper 3D vision, this method must replicate the object 4-6 times across the stereogram with little or no overlap. Hence the maximum width of the object is a fraction of the maximum width of the complete stereogram.

- For a sprite-based stereogram, the object is not replicated at all. Rather, individual pixels sampled from the background are selected and duplicated as needed. As a result, the object can occupy the entire width of the stereogram.

- Because this method replicates the object itself, the 3D effect is usually much cleaner and clearer than that obtained with a sprite-based stereogram, which almost randomly grabs background pixels.

The bottom line is that in practice we would almost never use this exact method. But there is a slight variation of this method that is enormously valuable.

Figure 33: Texture-mapped dragon with ivy texture

What makes this technique powerful is the fact that we can modify the reverse-overlaid texture of the object, making it slightly different from the background. Generally, we leave it close enough to the background that the object is difficult to discern with normal vision so as to keep the delicious element of surprise when it pops out at the observer in 3D vision. Also, and the main incentive for this section, is that by keeping the object's texture similar to the background, any occlusion due to overlap of instances is well disguised. But we make the object different enough from the background that when it is seen in 3D it stands out from the background more clearly than it would if its texture were identical to the background.

How do we slightly modify the object's texture? We could tweak its hue, or blur it, for example. But my favorite method is to do a transparent overlay of the original texture (Figure 30) onto the reverse-overlaid texture (Figure 32). Transparent overlays are discussed in detatil in the chapter on advanced techniques. For now, understand that it amounts to overlaying the original texture image onto the background in a way that makes it appear as if the overlay is partially transparent. The original shows up, but the background shows through the overlay as well.

I did this, created a single-object texture-mapped stereogram of the transparent overlay, and did a full overlay of that onto a flat stereogram of the background. I stitched some grassy ground onto the bottom of the image. Finally, I overlaid a multiple-object texture-mapped stereogram of a plant onto the whole thing. The result is shown in Figure 34. Note that in normal vision the presence of the dragon is visible, but its exact form is not. In 3D vision things become more clear.

Figure 34: Modified dragon texture stereogram

Outlining Objects on Sprite-Based Stereograms

An occasional problem with a sprite-based stereogram is that the exact shape of the object may not be as clearly defined as we wish. After all, unless we have highlighted a focus area as demonstrated with the diamond ring example (Figure 10), we get no help from the texture pattern. And even then, our only assistance is from whichever (usually minimal) area of focus is highlighted. The observer may get the general shape of the object, but inexperienced observers especially may have to do some guesswork to fully grasp the detailed structure of the object being displayed.

One approach to solving this problem is to outline the essential features of the object using fine lines that are in a color (usually very dark gray) that contrasts greatly with the background pattern. Create a single-object texture-mapped stereogram of this outline and overlay it onto the sprite stereogram. In the vast majority of situations, the object will occupy most of the width of the stereogram, so there will be enormous overlap and concomitant occlusion of the lines. As a result, the overlaid stereogram will contain not only the essential lines, but a large number of extraneous lines. Moreover, some of the lines will be incomplete at places where they are occluded. However, the human eye/brain is adept at ignoring these problems, due to the fact that the lines (if done correctly!) exactly demarcate the natural lines of the object. Because the lines are fine, they become a part of the background and, while quite visible, are generally accepted as just another aspect of the stereogram.

As a simple example, look at Figure 35 on the next page, which shows the depth map of a triangle rising up from the backplane, twisting as it rises. Figure 36 shows the essential lines of the object. (This figure is just for printing here. The actual texture map is very dark gray lines on a pure black background, making it almost impossible to see when printed.)

First I created an ordinary sprite-based stereogram of the depth image using a smoothly textured sprite. Then I created a single-object texture-mapped stereogram of the outline, using a depth map produced by masking the Figure 35 depth map with the Figure 36 'texture'. Finally I overlaid the latter stereogram onto the former. The result is shown in Figure 37. Note how the outline perfectly delineates the essential lines of the object, and in 3D vision the extraneous lines do not interfere.

This may not be the best example for demonstrating the technique, because the object is simple and easy to visualize. But for complex objects with numerous curves, the outlining technique can be wonderful.

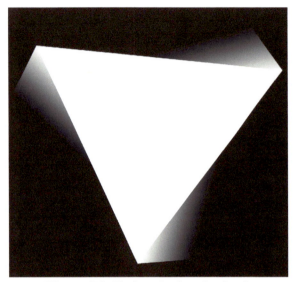

Figure 35: Twisted triangle depth

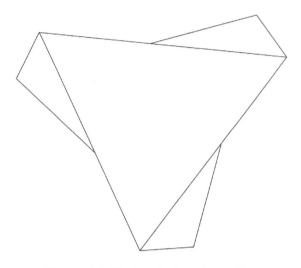

Figure 36: Twisted triangle outline

Figure 37: Final sprite stereogram with texture-mapped outline overlay

4

Advanced Stereogram Techniques

This chapter extends the prior chapter with techniques that enable the artist to create complex and beautiful stereograms.

Common Problems and Their Solutions

Most of the time, your first attempt at a stereogram project will result in significant ugliness. Especially for beginners, nothing ever goes right the first time. Weird echoes and artifacts appear in sprite-based stereograms. Black speckles appear in texture-based stereograms. Huge blocks of backplane instances of a single-object texture-mapped stereogram vanish, resulting in black swatches replacing the natural color of the instance. These sorts of problems are common as soon as you venture beyond the most elementary tasks. But please be aware that such problems are almost always solvable, and as you become more experienced you will learn how to prevent these problems in the initial design phase so that you don't have to go back later and fix things.

Artifacts in Sprite-Based Stereograms

As a general rule, sprite-based stereograms are much more forgiving and problem free than texture-mapped stereograms. This is largely because when stereogram pixels are undefined for some reason (this topic is discussed in detail in the programming section), all the program has to do is insert a reasonably intelligently selected background pixel. Thus, the undefined pixel will usually blend in with the natural background rather than being obtrusive.

The only serious problem that occasionally plagues sprite-based stereograms is accidental echoes that produce visible and annoying artifacts in 3D vision. Such artifacts are almost always invisible in normal vision, but when the observer switches to 3D vision, areas of the image may rise up from the background, creating false 'objects' in the image. They may rarely even appear to punch through the background and appear *behind* the backplane, or appear in front of or behind (in a punch-through) the correct object.

The root cause of this problem is rapid depth change that results in pixels with low Z that are near pixels with large Z being hidden from one or both eyes. This makes the low-Z pixels undefined, because a pixel must be visible to both eyes in order to have a defined color. As a result, the program selects background pixels to define the colors of the hidden pixels. In the programming section we'll discuss the exact algorithm by which the substitution is made; for now we'll consider the consequences and fixes.

A sure way to introduce ugly artifacts is to have pattern repetition *within* the basic background sprite. In most applications, the width of the background sprite will be exactly half the eye separation. For every row of this sprite image, there must be no visible duplication of a pattern. Some small duplication is almost impossible to avoid, and is usually inconsequential. But any duplication extensive enough to be visible is almost guaranteed to cause problems.

It is legal for the background sprite to be wider than half the eye separation; in fact, for focus preservation as in Figure 10, the width of the sprite must equal the full width of the stereogram. When the sprite is wider than half the eye separation, there must be no block of width equal to half the eye separation which contains visible repetition.

Even if there is no unwanted repetition within the sprite, ugly artifacts are possible. This is because the pixel substitution algorithm may accidentally produce unwanted pattern repetitions that simulate a small object that does not exist. Thus, the first line of attack should be to design the object in such a way that sudden depth changes, especially overhanging edges, are reduced or eliminated. Can the range of depth be reduced? Can the object be moved back toward the backplane, where pixel hiding is not as severe as when the object is close to the viewer? Having part of the object suddenly end, with an immediate plunge to the backplane, is very likely to cause problems. Whenever possible, taper the object smoothly to the backplane or a more distant part of the object. The operative word is *smooth*.

If sudden depth changes are intrinsic to the object, it may be possible to handle the problem with depth smoothing (*Image / Smooth Depth*). A very small row half-width, perhaps even 0, is usually fine. Most of the smoothing should be across columns. A good starting value for the column half-width is 1 percent of the stereogram width. Usually this will completely solve the problem, but fairly often the price will be too high by making unwelcome changes to the object in the form of visible ramps.

As a last resort, yet one that is often successful, twiddle with the eye separation. It is not unusual for an eye separation of, say, 1200 pixels to produce artifacts, while simply changing this to 1250 or 1150 pixels will remove the artifact. This is because the pixel substitution algorithm responsible for unwanted pattern repetition will change its substitution choices and thereby eliminate the accidental random repetition.

Black Speckles on Texture-Mapped Stereograms

Look at Figure 38, which shows a section of our lovely mermaid's tail on a single-object texture-mapped stereogram. On first thought it seems incredible that we would have hidden-pixel problems in a situation like this in which the depth changes slowly. Yet it can easily happen, so let's explore how it happens and how we can almost always fix it with little trouble.

Imagine that you are looking down at a staircase, directly above it. All stairs are in full view. Then you move back slightly. The front edge of each stair will now hide the back edge of the stair below. This hiding is the cause of speckling in a texture-based stereogram. The program colors undefined pixels as pure black, which lets the artist create a background onto which the texture-mapped stereogram can be overlaid in order to hide the problem. Of course, it's better to prevent the problem in the first place, rather than having to hide it, so...

If our hypothetical stairs are differing heights (different rates of depth change across the depth image), taller stairs (more rapid depth change) will cause more hiding, while shorter stairs may not hide anything at all. This often happens when depth images have been generated from discrete geometric shapes. Suppose that over 10 pixels the Z depth needs to change by 0.1. Ideally it should change by 0.01 per pixel. But the underlying geometry may actually change by the entire 0.1 in a single pixel and not change at all in the other 9 pixels due to the way the polygons are constructed. In this common situation, depth smoothing evens out the rate of depth change and will usually cure the problem completely. When you see the sort of banding displayed in Figure 38 you should always try depth smoothing first. Of course, this smoothing also causes ramps to form at places of large depth jumps, so be sure to examine the 3D image for ugly ramps.

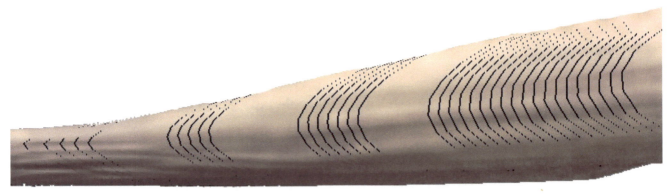

Figure 38: Staircase speckles due to discrete depth jumps

Almost always, column smoothing is more important than row smoothing. In fact, it is often the case that using a row half-width of 0, implying no row smoothing at all, is fine. I've never seen a situation in which a row half-width greater than 2 is needed. As a good rule of thumb, begin with a column half-width of about 1 percent of the total stereogram width. Reduce it as much as possible, or increase it if necessary. Experiment, and settle on the lowest half-width possible.

If smoothing is impossible due to the appearance of deal-killing ramps before the smoothing is sufficient to eliminate the speckling, or if smoothing helps greatly but does not quite solve the problem, try the *Attempt fixing hidden pixels* option in the stereogram generation menu. Sometimes this has an almost miraculous ability to fix speckling issues, while other times it makes the situation worse by introducing weird echoes in the stereogram. But never combine this option with oversampling, as the two algorithms are almost always incompatible.

The sort of speckling seen in Figure 38 can be caused by a completely different effect, and it requires a completely different solution. It may be that the depth changes rapidly but smoothly, with no individual depth change so large that pixel hiding occurs. However, as will be discussed in much more detail in the programming section, some stereogram pixels can still be undefined. The short version of the story is that distant parts of the object appear to be further apart as perceived by the left and right eyes than nearer parts of the object. If the depth of the object suddenly decreases from one object pixel to the next, even though the decrease may not be sufficient to cause hiding of nearby pixels, the perceived position of the object in terms of the observer's eyes may change by more than one pixel. In such a case, pixels in the observer's viewplane will be skipped and hence undefined.

The solution in this case is simple: oversampling. Each pixel in the object's texture image is replicated across the row, while the corresponding depth is interpolated. For example, suppose Z goes from 0.11 in one pixel to 0.16 in the next pixel. If we oversample by 5, our new, higher-resolution image will have 5 pixels with depths of 0.11, 0.12, 0.13, 0.14, and 0.15 for the first original pixel before jumping to 0.16 for the next pixel. We get 5 stereogram pixels which are averaged to produce a single stereogram pixel that corresponds to the original pixel. Actually it's not exactly that simple, but the details will have to wait for the programming section. This is the general idea, however. The bottom line is that in addition to, or instead of smoothing we may try oversampling. But note that when geometry is the primary source of the problem, oversampling can actually make the problem worse, and smoothing or hidden pixel fixing are the best options. Never combine oversampling with hidden pixel fixing, as the two algorithms tend to be incompatible.

It should be understood that the root cause of virtually *every* stereogram problem, whether it be occlusion due to overlap (discussed extensively in the prior chapter), or sprite-based stereogram artifacts, or hidden pixel speckling, or depth-change speckling, is overly rapid depth change. This can be especially problematic when the offending depth change is near the observer (large Z). This leads to some rules of thumb for reducing problems. Naturally, it may not always be possible to satisfy these rules. But it is always in the best interest of the artist to keep them in mind during the initial planning phases of a project.

- Keep the overall Z range of each individual object as small as possible. You can still obtain a huge total Z range for a project by placing limited-range objects on the stereogram using separate stereogram generation and overlays. For example, in an underwater scene you may have one type of fish with a Z range of 0.1 to 0.15, another at 0.3 to 0.35, and a third at 0.8 to 0.85. Don't even think about combining all three fish into a single texture image with an accompanying depth map having widely disparate depths. Instead, compute three separate stereograms, one for each fish, and then overlay them from most distant to closest. That way, each fish will have minimal depth change and hence minimal (if any!) problems, while the final stereogram will still have impressive depth variation.

- Hidden pixel problems are more severe near the observer (large Z) than further away. Thus, if you have an object that has a large depth range or sudden depth jumps, try to place it near the backplane (small Z) if possible.

- Especially for texture-mapped stereograms, avoid as much as possible poses in which part of the object is significantly in front of another part of the object. For example, look at Figure 24 and observe that the mermaid's right arm is in front of her body. That pose gave me fits because it generated numerous hidden pixels on the body at both edges of the arm. I had to use every trick in the book to clean that up. I did succeed, and I never had any doubts that I would be able to; these sorts of problems are only rarely unsolvable. But it was time consuming.

- For sprite-based stereograms, avoid if possible having the object end abruptly, with its depth going from a large Z to the backplane (Z=0) in one pixel. This invites problematic artifacts. Admittedly, this can be difficult, but it's worth keeping in mind to avoid fussing with eye separation to clean up ugly artifacts.

- In some applications it is beneficial to move up the backplane to a Z greater than 0. This very advanced topic is covered on Page 81.

Occlusion in Single-Object Texture-Mapped Stereograms

This topic has been dealt with extensively in prior sections, so I'll just summarize here. Occlusion happens when the object is so wide that its instances overlap. Occluded areas are undefined and hence made pure black so that the damaged stereogram can be overlaid onto a background that hopefully masks the problem. Please keep the following items in mind when designing your project:

- Overlap is not defined by the object's bounding box. Rather, it is defined line by line. Your goal is to provide a pose such that no individual line experiences overlap. For example, suppose your object is shaped like a 'less than' sign, <. A series of replications can be packed tightly and still have no overlap.

- In the final stereogram, never let the background for an occluded area be a solid color. That really makes the problem obvious.

- Try hard to match as closely as possible the color/texture of your background (that shows through the occluded area) and the object. Naturally there is a tradeoff here. You want the object to be distinct from the background in order to stand out clearly in 3D vision. So you have to compromise.

- Most of the techniques described in the prior section, such as oversampling, hidden pixel fixing, and smoothing, do nothing whatsoever to help occlusion from instance overlap. If you have overlap, the only thing that impacts the severity of the resulting occlusion is the difference between the depth at the edges of the object and the depth of the backplane (generally 0). So there are three things you can do in this regard:
  1) Move the object back as far as possible, close to the backplane.
  2) In special circumstances you can bring the backplane forward using *Adjust object*.
  3) If you can taper the edge of the object to the backplane, this will often solve the problem.

- In most cases, your only recourse is to intelligently and artistically design the background that will show through the occlusions when the stereogram is overlaid onto the background.

- Last but certainly not least, ponder long and hard whether you really need the object to be so wide that its instances overlap. Maybe you don't.

Transparent Overlays and Depth Splitting

Wonderful effects can be obtained by using transparent overlays, and it will often be the case that depth splitting will be a valuable tool for improving the appearance of transparent overlays. This section explores these two topics in a single project. Because this is a relatively complex project, we will work through it in detail, step-by-step. But before we begin, let's take a look at the final result, so we know what we are working toward. This is shown in Figure 39 below.

The pond has a green grassy bottom, and the surface appears as blue wispy ripples. The most difficult part of producing this image is making the line of toads at the top be partially submerged, with most of the body under the water, and the head above. Achieving this effect is the main goal of this example.

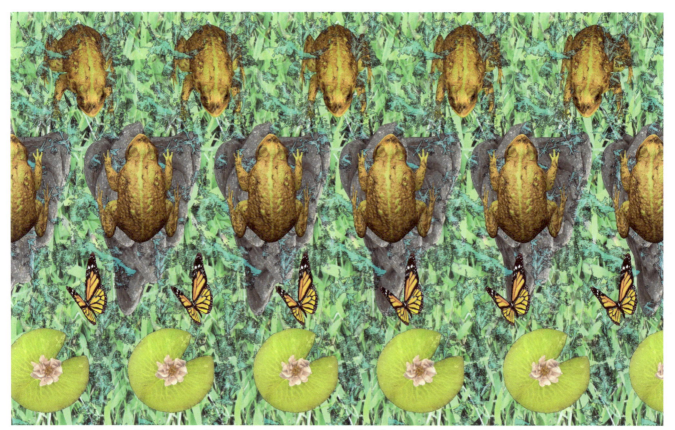

Figure 39: Transparent overlay and depth splitting demonstration

In most cases, a good first step is to produce the background that is on the backplane, and the transparent overlay. Water is a very common use for transparency, and it is also quite difficult. Despite being somewhat unrelated to reality, I chose to use densely matted grass for the pond bottom, and blue wisps for the surface, mainly because these colors and textures would contrast well with the objects in the scene. The sprites for these are shown in Figure 40 and Figure 41, respectively.

Before moving on to the objects in the scene, it is good to confirm the quality of the transparent overlay, tweaking it as necessary. In addition to making sure that the background and the overlay are sufficiently contrasting, there are two other parameters to consider. One is the depth of the overlay, the distance it lies above the background. Sometimes you will want it at the front, with Z=1 and all objects behind it. More often you will want it just a little in front of the background, far enough that depth is evident, but not so far that its relationship to the background is obscured. Here, I used Z=0.2.

The other parameter is the degree of transparency. The default of 0 makes the overlay completely opaque, with all non-black areas overwriting the background. The maximum of 100 makes it fully transparent and hence invisible and pointless. I used 50 percent here, which shows the overlay and the background equally. This is shown in Figure 42. You should not proceed until you are happy with this crucial foundation for your project.

Figure 40: Pond bottom

Figure 41: Pond surface

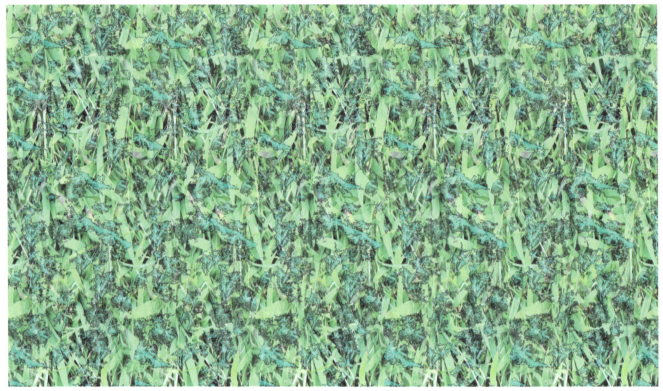

Figure 42: Pond bottom and surface

At this point it's tempting to just start depositing objects onto the background-plus-overlay scene. However, this usually will not give desirable results, because a direct overlay of an object will punch through the pond surface due to the object being a fully opaque overlay. The result is that the surface of the water will disappear above any part of the object that is below the water line, an odd and ugly appearance.

Unfortunately, the opposite order will not work either, unless the object is completely submerged. Suppose we were to overlay a relatively tall object onto the background and then do a transparent overlay of the water surface. The result would be the water surface mixing with the part of the object that is above water, giving a brain-boggling image in which the object itself appears transparent and we see the water surface inside of it! If you don't understand these two statements, try them yourself. You'll understand immediately.

The method for handling this issue for an object that lies both below and above the water surface is a little complex but effective. We use the *Split Object at Depth* operation to split the object at the depth of the water surface, and we create a stereogram of just the part of the object that is above the surface of the water. The toad was scaled to a Z range of 0 to 0.3. Figure 43 below shows the stereogram of the complete down-facing toad, and Figure 44 shows the corresponding stereogram of just the part of the toad that lies above Z=0.2, the water line. (Actually, both of these stereograms are the full size of the image, but the rest of the image is all black, so there's no point in wasting ink and paper by printing it here. So these figures are cropped.)

Figure 43: Complete toad, scaled for Z from 0 to 0.3

Figure 44: Part of toad that lies above Z=0.2, the water surface

The order of operation is now clear, and it follows the widely applicable rule of overlaying from back to front. First, overlay the complete toad onto the background, the pond bottom. Then do a transparent overlay of the water surface, which was created as a flat stereogram at Z=0.2. The result looks like Figure 45 on the next page. (Like the two figures above, the full image has been cropped to eliminate the uninteresting remainder.) Look at this image closely using 3D vision. Note how the water overlay covers the top of the toad, even though that part of the toad is above water. Bizarre! The brain doesn't know what to make of it.

The fix for this problem is simple: overlay the stereogram of the top of the toad, Figure 44. This overwrites the errant water surface pixels. If you look back at the top of Figure 39 you'll see how this completely solves the problem.

Figure 45:Background + complete toad + water surface confuses the brain before it's fixed

But we can't do those water surface and top-of-toad overlays quite yet, because we have the rock to deal with. It is scaled for Z from 0 to just barely less than 0.2 so that its top lies just below the water surface. That's not necessary, but it makes things easier by not requiring us to split the rock like we split the toad. So the exact steps so far are:

1) Load the pond bottom stereogram which forms the backplane
2) Overlay the complete small toad stereogram, which has Z from 0 to 0.3
3) Overlay the rock stereogram, which has Z from 0 to just under 0.2.
4) Do a 50% transparent overlay of the pond surface stereogram
5) Overlay the stereogram of the upper part of the down-facing toad, which has Z from 0.2 to 0.3.

With one anomalous exception, the remainder of the process is straightforward: compute and overlay stereograms of the upward-facing toad (Z from 0.2 to 0.5), the water lily (Z from 0.2 to 0.3), and the butterfly (Z from 0.9 to 1.0).

The one difficulty I encountered (and you may run into it as well) is that when I adjusted the Z range of the upward-facing toad to a minimum of 0.2, which should place the toad's feet on the rock and water surface, it was actually suspended noticeably above the water, floating in air! After some detective work, I discovered that the depth-generation program had the feet at Z=0.353 instead of 0, and there were one or more pixels of the texture that had a much smaller Z. Those erroneous pixels were scaled to Z=0.2, leaving the feet with a larger Z. This is clearly wrong, and it required me to fix it. So I used an external image editor to determine the real depth of the feet (Z=0.353). Then, when I adjusted the Z range with the *Adjust Object Size/Position* operation, I set the *Depth Floor* parameter to 0.353. This raised every smaller Z to this value, which is where the visible bottom of the toad is located, with the result that the feet are correctly rescaled to Z=0.2. The moral of the story is that you can never trust your image generation program!

Moving the Backplane Forward

When you create a single-object texture-mapped stereogram, the instances other than the focus object are spaced in such a way that in 3D vision they appear to lie on the backplane, which is most commonly Z=0. But if there is an object between the focus object and the backplane, and the instances of the focus object overlay the instances of the more distant object, a brain-confusing situation will result. The more distant object (but with Z>0) is 'in front of' the backplane (Z=0) instances of the focus object, and so in real life it would obscure those latter instances. But when we overlay the nearer (larger Z) single-object stereogram onto the more distant stereogram, the instances of the focus object will obscure the instances of the other object, exactly the opposite of what would happen in real life. The brain does not know how to handle this, and the result is inability to form proper 3D vision. This problem can come about in many ways when stereograms of different depths are overlaid in improper order, but the problem is most common and serious for a single-object stereogram due to that fact that only the focus instance is in front of the backplane; all other instances are at the backplane. Thus, these other instances, having Z=0, can easily fall behind an object that is in front of them, while simultaneously obscuring them rather than being obscured.

The solution is simple: when we create the single-object stereogram, we move its backplane forward with the *Backplane Z* entry in the *Adjust Object Size/Position* command. Of course, we should have some sort of barrier at the new backplane, or the other instances will appear to float in space, something that is not disastrous but is usually unpleasant. A nice side-effect of doing this is obtained if our object is so large that overlap of instances happens. Recall that the degree of horrible occlusion resulting from overlap depends on how far the object is from the backplane. If we move the backplane up close to the overlapped object, the degree of occlusion is usually reduced by an enormous amount.

To create this demonstration I produced a sky-with-clouds sprite and generated a flat stereogram at Z=0. For interest I created a multiple-object stereogram of a tree with a Z range of 0.1–0.2 and overlaid it onto the sky scene. Then I used a photograph of an apartment front as a sprite to create a flat stereogram with Z=0.8 and overlaid it. I created two different single-object stereograms of a runner and overlaid each onto the sky/tree/apartment scene. For the overlay shown in Figure 46 I left the runner's backplane at its default (and most common value) of Z=0. Notice how it is impossible to achieve proper 3D vision with this image, due to the conflict arising from non-focus instances of the runner appearing at the Z=0 backplane despite occluding the Z=0.8 apartment front. Figure 47 shows the scene when the runner's stereogram is generated with the backplane at Z=0.8, the same depth as the apartment front, thus eliminating any conflict.

Figure 46: Runner stereogram backplane is incorrectly set at Z=0, causing confusion

Figure 47: Runner stereogram correctly has backplane at apartment front

Placing Objects on a Horizontal Surface

Sometimes you want to have a horizontal surface extending outward toward the observer, and place one or more objects on it. The most common use of this technique is to have the observer at or just above ground level, looking toward the horizon, and seeing a landscape arrayed in front of the sky backplane above the land. The difficulty level of this important technique ranges from almost trivial to nearly impossible, depending on how you design the layout. For a crude introduction to the relevant issues, I created a background sprite whose upper half is a cloudy sky and whose lower half is a grassy surface, as shown in Figure 48. The corresponding depth map, Figure 49, has the upper half at Z=0, while the lower half linearly moves to Z=1.

Figure 48: Sprite for surface demo

Figure 49: Depth map for surface demo

Figure 50 shows a tall, thin planar object (not yet expanded to the full stereogram width), and its depth map in Figure 51 places the object at a constant Z=0.5. Figure 52 on the next page shows the corresponding stereogram in the multiple-object version. (Single-object stereograms do not work well with placement on a surface because only the primary instance looks correct. All other instances appear on the Z=0 backplane and hence below the surface, which greatly disturbs the brain in 3D vision.) Note the following:

- The objects pierce downward through the grassy surface, an almost always undesirable effect.

- If you look at the top half only, the object correctly appears to be perfectly vertical.

- If you look at the bottom half only, the object appears to slant backwards, away from the 'front' of the scene, because the viewpoint seems to be looking downward at an angle.

Figure 50: Tall object

Figure 51: Depth map

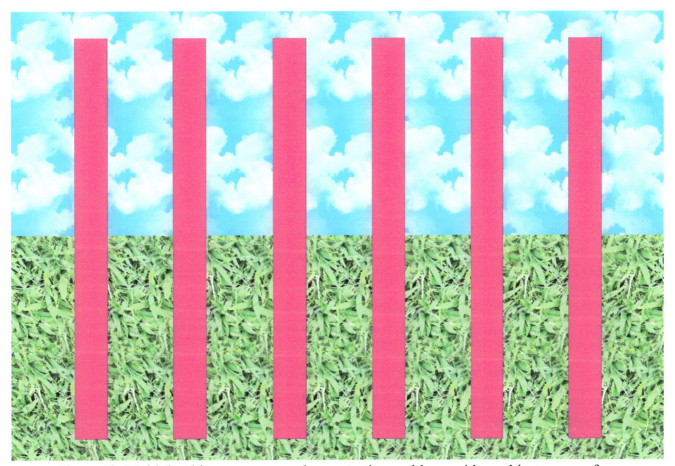

Figure 52: Multiple-object stereogram demonstrating problems with an object on a surface

One obvious take-away from this demonstration is that different rules apply for parts of an object above and below the horizon. Thus, ***we should strenuously avoid having an object extend vertically across significant spans on BOTH sides of the horizon (above and below).*** If the object has to be tall, extending well up into the Z=0 background, it should be far back on the horizontal surface, near the horizon. Similarly, objects near the observer (near the bottom of the image, where Z approaches 1.0) should have little or no extension up into the Z=0 background area.

A more difficult issue is that to prevent objects from piercing through the horizontal surface as seen here, or mysteriously floating above the ground, we have some work to do.

Calculating Correct Placement Coordinates

If the object is fairly short and has a narrow bottom, such as a plant or a very small object, correct placement is simple. (For this reason, we should always attempt to limit ourselves to small or narrow-bottomed, short objects!) We just use ordinary linear interpolation to find the row in the stereogram at which we must place the bottom of our object in order for it to exactly rest on the horizontal surface. In particular, if we define quantities as shown below, Equation (4.1) gives the row number at which the bottom of the object must be placed. We'll see an example of this calculation on Page 89.

Z - The Z coordinate of the bottom of the object, which must exactly touch the horizontal surface.

Z_0 - The Z at the back of the horizontal surface, typically but not necessarily 0, the grand backplane.

Z_1 - The Z at the front of the horizontal surface, typically but not necessarily 1.

R_0 - The row number at the back of the horizontal surface; the bottom-most row of the Z_0 backplane.

R_1 - The row number of the front of the horizontal surface, typically but not necessarily the bottom row of the stereogram.

$$Row = R_0 + (Z - Z_0) / (Z_1 - Z_0) * (R_1 - R_0) \tag{4.1}$$

Tall Vertical and Flat-Bottomed Objects

Suppose we have an object that traverses a significant number of rows of the horizontal surface and that is tall enough that the observer can discern whether it is tilted forward or backward of truly vertical. Or suppose the object has a large flat bottom that extends a significant distance in the Z direction and for which we can see not only the front but the back of the bottom as well. In either case, we're toast. Well, not exactly, but almost. We can usually work around it, though only with considerable effort or compromise. This should be strong motivation to avoid such situations in our design. But if our art concept demands either of these situations, we now explore how to tackle it.

First of all, here are some important critical concepts:

- The worst possible situation is when you have an object that has a clearly preferred Z orientation, such as a tree or flagpole that most observers would expect to be upright rather than slanted toward or away from the observer, AND it is in the foreground, meaning that it traverses a large fraction of the horizontal surface, AND the horizontal surface occupies many rows of the stereogram, AND the object is so tall that it crosses above the horizon into the backplane. In this rare situation (rare because you make it rare!), you are in a tough spot. Going from bottom to top, you can pull Z away from the backplane until it hits the horizon, but the calculations involved are impractically complex. I wish I could be more help for this one, but it is really tough. You literally have to bend the object at the horizon, and the techniques described soon may help, but you will almost surely tear out all of your hair before giving up in dismay.

- The best solution, which basically solves all problems, is to use just a small fraction of the height of the stereogram to span the horizontal surface. This corresponds to the observer being practically at ground level, in which case distortions due to a higher apparent viewpoint are almost entirely eliminated. Vertical still looks vertical, even as it traverses the horizontal surface. Flat-bottomed objects appear to sit entirely on the surface as long as they are not too far off-kilter. The stereogram just shown in Figure 52 is an extreme example of how *not* to do it. The short grassy extent in Figure 34 on Page 66, and the ocean bottom in Figure 25 on Page 58, are reasonable approaches that usually require nothing more than the use of Equation (4.1) to place the object with its bottom on the correct row for it's Z coordinate.

- If your problem is that the bottom of the object is not sitting evenly on the horizontal surface, you can usually solve the problem with the technique described soon. But you are better off avoiding that messy work entirely. Can you rotate the object in such a way that the back of its bottom does not show? Then all you have to do is use Equation (4.1) to correctly position the front of the bottom, and you don't have to worry about the back. For example, suppose your object is a pyramid. Positioning it with the corner in front means that the other two back corners show clearly and need special accommodation. But if you position the flat surface in front, with the left and right front corners at the same Z coordinate, the back corner will be hidden and can be ignored.

If you absolutely *must* have an extensive horizontal surface, and your object is either tall (so tilting is obvious) and/or wide-bottomed (so it has to sit flat on the surface), you have some tedious work to do. When you create the texture and depth images in your graphics program, you will have to place the camera not just in front of the object as is usual practice, but also raised up above the horizon, looking down on the object at an angle.

On first thought it would seem that one could easily compute the exact angle at which to look down on the object. After all, rows in the stereogram map to Z coordinates of the object. One could compute the ratio of the vertical change in row to the horizontal change in Z and use simple trigonometry to find the apparent look-down angle. Unfortunately, it's far from that simple. The aspect ratio when printing comes into play. And how do Z distances and row distances map to actual physical distance units that define the object? And how does the range of Z in the graphics program relate to the 0-1 range of Z in stereogram generation? And what if you are adjusting Z with the *Adjust Object Size/Position* command, which you likely will do? The number of variables involved makes calculation of an exact camera lookdown angle impossible.

The only way to tackle this problem, at least as far as I have found, is trial and error. Be sure that you have a way to display the stereogram in the size you will use when printing, so you can properly judge the appearance in 3D vision. Raise the camera moderately above the horizon and grab depth and texture images. Make the stereogram of the object, overlay it onto the background/surface stereogram, and see how it looks. Then raise or lower the camera by what seems to be a reasonable amount and try again. Repeat as needed. As long as no foreground objects are so tall that they cross above the horizon boundary, you will be able to find a good solution. You can also make fine adjustments to the position by moving the object up and down slightly on the stereogram; moving it up (higher; smaller row number) raises it further relative to the horizontal surface. But such movement may not be appropriate for your artistic design, and your only choice may be manipulating the camera in the projection software.

An Example of a Difficult Situation

In this section I present an example of exactly the sort of situation that should be avoided if possible, because handling it well is tedious and difficult. There are two root causes of the problem demonstrated here:

1) The horizontal surface has a large extent; half of the stereogram rows (1000 of 2000) are dedicated to the surface. It's always easiest when the surface rows are a small fraction of the total number of rows, because then the lookdown angle is practically zero, and errors in such a tiny lookdown angle are hard to see. With the substantial lookdown angle in this demonstration, even small errors are painfully visible in 3D vision. Your depth and texture generation needs to be practically perfect.

2) Both objects in this demonstration have visible areas near the front and back that must exactly touch the surface. If these areas pierce below the surface or float above it, these errors will be obvious to the observer in 3D vision (though completely invisible in normal vision!).

To begin, I took two photos of old wood planks in a building, each 600 columns wide by 1000 rows high. Stitching them together vertically gave the 600 x 2000 background sprite shown in Figure 53. I created the stereogram background by using the *Make Depth Backplane* function with parameters (0,0), (50,0), (100,100). This places the upper half of the sprite at Z=0 and tapers the bottom half linearly from 0 to 1.

Figure 54 shows a cat object (the actual background is black, but I made it white for display here to save black ink), and Figure 55 shows a mouse. I made multiple-object stereograms of both of them and overlaid them onto the background.

The cat was a little easier than the mouse because the lowest (maximum row) is the cat's front-left foot, which of course has to touch the floor. When the extreme bottom (row-wise) of the object is at ground level, the situation is relatively easy because we can explicitly compute the bottom row for placement of the object with the *Adjust Object Size/Position* command. In this case I used an external image editor with the depth image to determine that for the bottom of that foot, Z=0.447. I rescaled the depth to a maximum (which occurs at the left ear) of 0.6, so the actual Z of that paw is 0.447 * 0.6 = 0.268. Equation (4.1) on Page 86 tells us that the bottom of the object, this paw, must be placed at row 1000 + 0.268 * 1000 = 1268.

Figure 53:
Sprite

Figure 54: Cat object

Figure 55: Mouse object

When I placed it there, created the multiple-object stereogram, and overlaid it onto the background stereogram, I was overjoyed. The back-right foot was pretty close to the floor, just sunk a little below it. My initial guess for the camera lookdown angle had been good, so I did not have to go through the tedium of repositioning the camera and recreating the texture and depth images. All I needed to do was slightly adjust the upper row of the cat object, leaving the bottom row at its perfectly computed location. When you move an object upward (smaller row number) in the stereogram, it rises relative to the floor. (If this is not clear, think hard about it, as it is a crucial concept.) So some minor tweaking of the upper row was all that was needed to fix the situation. Of course, this does slightly alter the aspect ratio of the object as well as its position on the stereogram. In some applications either or both of these side effects would be intolerable and you would have to adjust the camera. Luckily, these made no difference in this demonstration, so making the cat stand perfectly on the floor was easy.

The mouse was somewhat more difficult, because the tip of the tail, the bottom-most row in the image, does not sit on the floor; it is raised up a little. Rather, we have to deal with the two right feet. Equation (4.1) does us no good other than providing a rough starting guess based on the tip of the tail. But again I was lucky because my initial guess for the camera position was close enough that I could go with it.

All I needed to do was adjust the upper and lower extent of the mouse object in order to get both feet precisely on the floor. This was a bit tiresome, because since the feet are both in the interior of the object, the top and bottom rows impact both feet. I had to do a lot of twiddling with the placement to get it right, but it happened eventually. The final result is shown in Figure 56.

Figure 56: Final cat-and-mouse stereogram

Extreme Overlap

Sometimes you desperately want to have a single texture-mapped object extend across most of the width of your stereogram. In such a situation, extreme overlap is unavoidable. For an example of such a situation, look at Figure 57 below. There are four important principles to keep in mind when you have extensive overlap:

- If part of the object is especially important, try to have it above or below other parts of the object so that it does not suffer occlusion or texture distortion from averaging in texture from another part of the object. In Figure 57 I managed to get most of the head isolated.

- Occlusion is worst when Z is large, so try to isolate high-Z parts of the object, and have most of the overlap occur in low-Z areas. In Figure 57 the head is nearest the observer and also most isolated. Most overlap involves the tail, and it is near the backplane (low Z). This is good.

- The object should be as uniform in color as possible so that averaging in overlapped areas does not look weird. Note how the tip of the tail gets averaged in with the neck. Imagine how strange this would look if the tail and the neck were dramatically different colors. This is bad enough.

- The background color should be close to the object's color so that when it shows through in occlusions it attracts as little attention as possible.

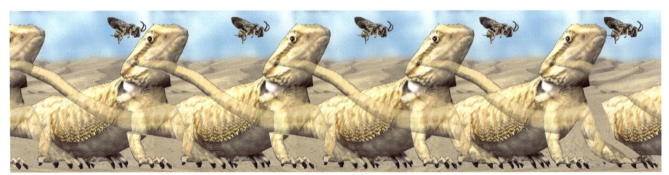

Figure 57: Demonstration of extreme overlap

Let's now look at how Figure 57 was constructed. As is common, I began by creating the single-object stereogram of the lizard. Not surprisingly, there was relatively little occlusion to the left of the object, because that part has low Z. But the occlusion from the head, which is closest to the observer, is enormous. Look at how much is missing from the body of the rightmost instance. In my original design, I had the lizard slightly to the left of center, which gave a lovely effect. But then the two instances to its right were massively occluded. So I changed my plan and slid it to the right enough that only one instance was occluded. There are multiple instances to its left, but because the tail is near the backplane they suffered very little occlusion.

Also note that I adjusted the eye spacing so that the tail ends at exactly the edge of the neck. Having a little stub of tail stick out of the left side of the neck does not harm the stereo image at all, but it looks really silly!

Once the lizard stereogram was complete, I could design the background. Sand dunes are a great complement, both because this is (I think?) a reasonably natural looking habitate for the lizard, and the color match is also good. So I created a background image in which the dunes came up just high enough to obscure head occlusion by the tail. Then I tacked on a bit of cloudy sky on top.

I also tacked on a very few rows of sand surface at the bottom to give the lizard something to be standing on. The following backplane parameters gave the perfect depth map for the background, which is created as a sprite-based stereogram.

```
0      0
96.67  0
100  100
```

All that's left is to overlay the lizard onto the background, and overlay a multiple-object bee onto it for interest. I took care to position the bee left-right in such a way that it did not overwrite any part of the lizard's head.

Last but not least, I will confess that I did a little cleanup work with an external image editor. Although the tail did almost no obscuring of the body on the left side, it did leave a thin little line in which the sand background showed through. I used an editor to copy lizard texture onto those few thin lines. This would be very bad to do if there was massive obscuring, because the brain knows that obscured parts are truly hidden, and it becomes confused when it sees part of the object. But tiny touch-ups like this are fine.

A Complex Hybrid Stereogram

This final demonstration puts together most of the concepts we've explored individually. These include, in a single stereogram image:
- A sprite-based stereogram
- Overlaid single-object stereograms
- Overlaid multiple-object stereograms
- Stereograms based on 3D objects
- Stereograms based on flat-depth objects
- Manual depth splitting to handle one object spanning another object in depth
- Transparent overlays

Because this project is so complex, I'll describe each step in great detail. But first, let's look at the final product, shown in Figure 58.

Figure 58: Multiple techniques in a single stereogram

The first step in any stereogram project is to decide on the display size of the dominant object(s). Clearly, the swimmer is the primary object in this scene, with the shark being a close second. Everything else is just decoration. The texture and depth images of the swimmer are 2200 by 1000. All stereograms in this book are 7 inches wide, and I generally shoot for about 5 (4.5–6, actually) replications at the backplane. If we go toward the low end, objects will be larger, which is always nice. Using the 'standard' eye separation of 2.5 inches gives 2 * 7 / 2.5 = 5.6 replications (the 2 is because the eye separation is twice the replication width, as discussed several times earlier). But the human eye easily accommodates modest deviation from this standard, so an eye spacing of 3 inches is perfectly reasonable. This gets us nicely down to 4.67 replications.

As a quick initial ballpark figure, consider that because the swimmer is somewhat in front of the backplane, she will have a few more replications than the background, perhaps about 5. If she were not able to overlap and we wanted to retain her full raw resolution (always good when possible) we would need a horizontal resolution of 2200 * 5 = 11,000 pixels, a rather extreme quantity. But because her right arm is well above her feet, considerable overlap is possible without occlusion. Very little experimentation was needed to confirm that a width of 7000 pixels, with an eye spacing of 3000 pixels (7000 pixels / 7 inches * 3 inches), gives only slight occlusive overlap, and in the final adjustment we can shrink it a little as needed to remove this overlap. This is still a little excessive in terms of memory and time resources, as it provides a resolution of 1000 pixels per inch, well beyond the more common printing resolution 300 dots per inch. But I did not want to reduce the resolution of the swimmer much, so I went with it.

Such convenient overlap is not possible with the shark, so I know I'll have to reduce its size, while still leaving it as large as possible, keeping it just under the point of overlap. For the moment I just expanded it to 7000 columns to match the swimmer and noted modest but not extreme overlap, well withing the range of what can be done with adjustment while not losing much resolution. All other objects in the scene are just decoration and can be completely ignored for now. The horizontal size is taken care of.

As is almost always the case, vertical sizing is much more difficult. A large sketch is a helpful tool. In this case, I drew two horizontal lines, well spaced, to represent the net height of the swimmer, 1000 rows. We want the chin to be just above the water line, a natural swimming position. By expanding the image to the full monitor height, measuring down to the millimeter, and using ratios, I determined that there would be 410 rows above and 1000-410=590 rows below. This does not have to be a final figure, as small adjustments later are easy. We just need something close for now. So I drew a horizontal line approximately proportioned to represent the water line as her chin.

I wanted the shark to be immediately below the swimmer, with no intervening gap (a purely artistic decision), and the shark image is 1000 rows high at full resolution. Again, we can do minor adjustment of the shark's position later, but for overall sizing we can plan to make the total height of the underwater part be the underwater part of the swimmer, 590 rows, plus the shark's height, 1000 rows. Thus, the underwater section of the stereogram will contain 1590 rows.

Naturally, we don't want the upper part of the swimmer just hanging in thin air. At a minimum she needs a background behind her. Moreover, some sky overhead would be nice. The amount of sky (number of rows) is a purely artistic decision. We want enough for good context and maybe some decoration, but not so much that it overshadows the main components of the scene, the swimmer and the shark. Recall that 410 rows are taken up by the upper part of the swimmer. Given that the below-water part is 1590 rows, I decided that a total of 1200 rows above water would be good, large but noticeably less than the below-water part. This would allow 1200-410=790 rows of clear air above the swimmer, which seems good (but is not a magic number, just a personal artistic judgement). This gives us a final sum of 1590+1200=2790 rows for the stereogram image (and the 7000 columns we already decided on).

It's a nice touch in such situations to show the water surface. On the other hand, this can be tricky for two reasons. One reason is that if we show more than a tiny amount of surface, we have to deal with raising the camera angle as discussed in the "Placing Objects on a Horizontal Surface" on Page 83. By keeping the amount of surface small, we can get away with a simple direct camera angle. The other problem is that the swimmer does have a Z direction, and if the amount of water surface is large we have to deal with depth splitting (Page 76) any time the swimmer and the surface cross over each other. If we keep the water surface small, we can get away with a single depth split, the row at which her head lies directly above the water. There may still be errors, but they should be so small that they are effectively invisible.

Thus, I chose to make the water surface cover an even 100 rows. The swimmer's neck is at approximately Z=0.6, so assuming that the water Z runs from 0 to 1, there will need to be 60 rows of water surface behind (above in the stereogram) the swimmer, and 40 rows in front (below in the stereogram). We will create a band of 60 rows of water surface texture and depth, ranging from Z=0 to Z=0.6, with its bottom row being 1200. We similarly create a band of 40 rows of water surface texture and depth, ranging from Z=0.6 to Z=1.0, with its top row being 1201. In both cases, we will stitch solid black rows above and below the band to create a sprite that is the same height as the stereogram, 2790 rows, and with a width equal to half the eye separation, 3000/2=1500 columns.

We can use the same depth map for both, employing the *Make Depth Backplane* function with the following parameters:

0	0.0
40.860	0.0
44.440	100.0
44.49	0.0
100	0.0

It's fine to use this same depth image for both because each depth image is used only in its non-black texture parts. Parts of the depth map in a black portion of the texture map of the water surface are ignored. The last step in creating the water surface is to, for each part (behind and in front), make a sprite-based stereogram that we save and set aside for later.

We now need to temporarily put the important parts together and do a small amount of experimentation. Make a 1500 by 1200 sky sprite consisting of a blue sky and some puffy white clouds, and use the *Flat Stereo Image* function to create a 7000 by 1200 sky background, which you should save for later. Also make a 1500 by 1590 underwater sprite (make it pretty!), and use the *Flat Stereo Image* function to create a 7000 by 1590 underwater background at Z=0. Save this, as you will need it soon for dealing with the shark. Stitch these together with an external image editor to make a single 7000 by 2790 stereogram consisting entirely of background. Save this, as you will need it for positioning the swimmer.

Expand the swimmer to 7000 columns by 2790 rows and make a single-image stereogram which you temporarily overlay onto the background just created. Now repeatedly use the *Adjust Object Size/Position* command to move her around until she's just right. Each time you will need to re-read the background to clear out the overlay, and redo the stereogram. It's critical that the base of her chin end up barely above the water/air interface. If you want her swimming to the left, as I did, she should be positioned slightly to the right of center. I also adjusted her Z range to 0.4–0.7, which seems reasonable. She needed to be smoothed 70 by 1 to eliminate step occlusion (see Figure 38 on Page 72).

The shark is trickier because it is a hybrid of a single-object-texture-mapped stereogram and a sprite-based stereogram. Begin with the texture-mapped version. Expand its texture and depth to the underwater stereogram's 7000 by 1590, create the stereogram, and overlay it onto the underwater stereogram you just created. (I hope you saved that to a file, as you will need to keep restoring it as you experiment.) I used the *Adjust Object Size/Position* command to place the bottom of the shark almost at the bottom of the stereogram, and its top just barely below where the bottom of the swimmer will be. (The swimmer is not present here yet, but you should be able to calculate closely enough with rulers and ratios.) Make its horizontal size in proportion to its vertical size and position it such that no instance of its top fin overlaps where the swimmer's bottom arm will be, with the overall shark somewhat left of center. (You may need to come back to this step later and fix it if you miscalculated.) I set its Z range to 0.5–0.7. When you have it perfectly positioned, take note of the vertical and horizontal positions in case you need to redo things with more minor adjustments.

The next few steps are tricky, using some of the most sophisticated tricks in the *Stereo* program. Load the 7000 by 1590, Z=0 underwater background you created earlier into the *Sprite* area. The final depth image that you created as part of the recent adjustment process is critical, because you will soon use that same depth image to create the shark's sprite-based stereogram. Load the shark's expanded and adjusted texture into an external image editor. Blacken the entire shark image except the teeth and a small perimeter of the mouth. Save this to serve as a focus area and then read it into a work area in *Stereo*. Now overlay this with 50 percent transparency (an arbitrary value determined by artistic choice) onto the *Sprite*. In the external editor, remove the red component of this remaining image, leaving just the blue and black components. Draw a vertical red line through the approximate center of the mouth-tooth area. Read this image into *Work1*, with the depth image still in *Depth*. Use the *Work1 Red to Depth* command, which will copy the red line in *Work1* to the depth image, thus defining the focus area.

At this time you have the underwater section ready to go. The mouth/teeth texture image has been transparently overlaid onto the *Sprite* full background, and the entire depth image with its vertical red focus line is in the *Depth* area. Create a Sprite-based stereogram. The result will be a shark that, except for the mouth and teeth, is invisible in normal vision, but which will pop out dramatically in stereo vision.

You may wish to stop at this point, leaving the bulk of the shark invisible in normal vision to increase the drama when the observer sees it. In fact, overlaying the mouth/teeth in a higher transparency (or not overlaying it at all!) will make that drama even more profound. But I prefer to make things a little easier for the observer. To do this, I overlaid onto this sprite stereogram the previously created single-object stereogram of the shark, but using a very high transparency (70 percent). In normal vision, the shark appears as a vague shadow, and in stereo vision it really jumps out at the observer. This hybrid of transparently overlaying a single-object texture-mapped stereogram onto a sprite-based stereogram can be powerful.

The sky section is a lot easier. As the first step, you created a flat stereogram (Z=0) consisting of blue sky and some puffy clouds. Now get an image of a few flat (not 3D) seagulls, expand them to a sprite of 1500 by 1200, and create a flat stereogram with Z=0.2 (slightly in front of the cloud background). Adjust their size and position so that they complement the clouds. When their stereogram is perfect, overlay it onto the sky/cloud stereogram to make the above-ground stereogram.

At last it's time to put everything together. Stitch the above-surface stereogram just created onto the underwater (including shark) stereogram laboriously created a moment ago. Overlay the back-of-water-surface onto this, confirming once again that the bottom row of this corresponds to the bottom row of the above-surface stereogram. This overlay is the part of the water surface that lies behind the swimmer. Overlay the swimmer stereogram (expanded to 7000 by 2790) onto this, and overlay the front-of-water-surface next, again confirming that its top row exactly touches the bottom row of the back part.

The rest is trivial decoration. I created a couple of flat (not 3D) fish. In each case, expand them to 7000 by 2790, use the *Make Depth Backplane* function to create flat depth images at Z=0.8 and Z=0.9 respectively, use the *Mask Depth from Texture* function, and create a multiple-object stereogram of each. Overlay them after suitable adjustment of size and position. Do the same with the hot-air ballon, which I set at Z=0.4. Voila! Complete.

5

The Sprite Stereogram Algorithm

This chapter presents the algorithm for creating sprite-based stereograms, along with complete source code. This code is in the file M3D_1.CPP which can be downloaded for free from the author's website. Please note that this routine is (in theory!) written in such a way that the sprite and depth images can be either 8-bit black-and-white or 24-bit full color. However, the *Stereo* program requires that all images be 24-bit, so the 8-bit options in this code have not been thoroughly tested.

Terminology

The following terminology will appear in this discussion:

- The **backplane** is the furthest that any part of the object can be from the eyes, and it corresponds to a depth of Z=0.

- The **viewplane** is where the stereogram is projected, typically a computer monitor or a printed page. The viewplane lies exactly halfway between the eyes and the backplane, because the mathematics is easiest when we place it here.

- The Greek letter **mu** (μ) is the maximum fraction 0–1 of the backplane–viewplane distance that the object can traverse toward the eyes. The standard default is to set *mu*=1/3, meaning that the closest that any part of the object can be to the eye is one-third of the way from the backplane to the viewplane. This corresponds to a depth of Z=1.0. Larger values provide more profound 3D effects but are also more difficult for many people to visualize.

- We have a **depth image** that defines the depth dimension of the object. The computed stereogram will have the same row and column dimensions as the depth image. Mathematically, the depth ranges from Z=0 (the backplane) to 1 (a distance of mu times the backplane-viewplane distance). This range is represented as a grayscale range of 0–255, with Z=tone/255. If the depth image is 24-bit color, the tone is defined as the mean of the green and blue channels, with the red channel playing no role in depth. The *Stereo* program always makes the green and blue channels equal.

- If the depth image is 24-bit color, the red channel defines the **focus column**. For any row, the rightmost column that has the red channel equal to 128 or more is considered the center of the area of interest (the focus) for that row. When several columns are constrained to be the same color, whichever column is closest to the focus determines the common color. If no column has the red channel greater than or equal to 128, the focus is assumed to be the center column.

- The *eye separation* is the number of columns between the left and right eyes. When the stereogram is displayed on a monitor or printed, this is usually about 2.5 inches, although anything in the range of 2–3 inches is acceptable for most observers.

- The *sprite* is the image from which stereogram colors will be obtained. It usually has the same number of rows as the depth image, although if it has fewer rows it will be repeated vertically as needed, and if it has more rows, the extra rows at the bottom will be ignored. When no area of focus is involved, the sprite will almost always have a number of columns equal to half of the eye separation, and there will be a smooth pattern transition when it is horizontally tiled. When there is an area of focus, the sprite must have the same number of rows and columns as the depth image, and in nearly all such situations the sprite will have been created by horizontal tiling (with smooth transitions) of an image having its number of columns equal to half the eye separation. In other words, a full-width sprite will be horizontally periodic with period equal to half the eye separation. This is not mandatory, and failing to satisfy this periodicity will not damage the 3D effect, but it will usually make the normal-vision stereogram less pretty.

- *FAR* is half of the eye separation, and this is the horizontal repetition period at the backplane. In other words, at the backplane (Z=0), columns separated by a distance of FAR will be constrained to be identical. This will be more clear when we examine Equation (5.2) on Page 104. This is why the sprite nearly always is designed to be FAR columns wide or repeat internally at this rate. This makes background areas have a pleasantly smooth repetition rather than having jarring discontinuities.

- *NEAR* is the horizontal repetition period when Z=1, the closest that the object can be. It is always less than FAR and depends on the eye separation and mu. It is discussed more in the next section, and defined in Equation (5.3) on Page 106.

Because column locations on the stereogram are integers, the possible depths that can be displayed are discrete. In particular, we can display FAR–NEAR+1 different depths because there are this many integers between NEAR and FAR, inclusive of those values.

Geometry and Key Equations

Please look at Figure 59 on the next page. The vertical direction in this illustration represents columns going across a single row. The profile of the object being viewed is portrayed with a bold outline at the right side of the figure. The left and right eyes, at the far left side of the figure, are separated by *Eye* columns. We are looking directly at a point A on the object that is midway between the eyes. (This positioning is the usual assumption, and the parallax error when this is not the case is generally inconsequential and can be ignored to keep the math simple.) This point A is at a depth of Z_0.

The *viewplane*, which is the surface on which we perceive the stereogram (typically a computer monitor or printed page) is shown as a vertical line in the center of the figure. There are two types of measurement in the horizontal (depth) direction on this figure. Z is a dimensionless quantity that represents the distance between the observer and a point on the object. It ranges from 0 at the backplane, the maximum distance from the observer, to 1, which is the closest any point on the object can come to the observer. The horizontal direction in the figure also represents distance as measured in *units*, where 1 unit is defined as the distance between the eyes and the viewplane, as well as the distance between the viewplane and the backplane.

The user-specified quantity *mu* is the maximum distance in units between the backplane and the viewplane that the object can span. In the upper-right corner of the figure we see that span represented by a vertical line *mu* units in front of the backplane in which Z ranges from 0 to 1. It should be apparent that the distance in units of any point on the object from the backplane is *mu* times Z. From this, the two distances shown at the bottom of the figure follow directly: the distance in units between point A on the object and the viewplane is $1 - mu\, Z_0$ and the distance between point A on the object and the eye plane is $2 - mu\, Z_0$.

The most important computation is the position of point D on the viewplane, the number of columns separating it from point B. Because both eyes are seeing the same point, A, we must color point D (what the left eye sees) and its symmetric buddy G an equal distance on the other side of point B (what the right eye sees) the same. The triangle defined by A–B–D and that defined by A–C–*LeftEye* are similar (same angles), so the simple ratio shown in Equation (5.2) gives the number of columns defined by B–D.

$$B - D = \frac{\left(1 - \mu Z_0\right)}{\left(2 - \mu Z_0\right)} * Eye\, /\, 2 \tag{5.2}$$

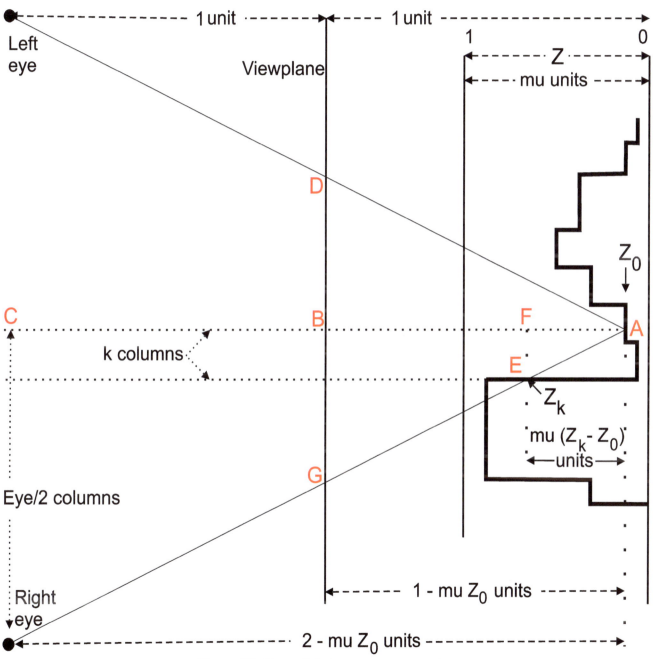

Figure 59: Essential stereogram geometry

Equation (5.2) easily gives the repetition period (G–D) at the nearest distance (Z=1), as shown in Equation (5.3).

$$NEAR = \frac{(1 - \mu)}{(2 - \mu)} * Eye \tag{5.3}$$

Life being what it is, there can be a complication. In Figure 59 we see that part of the object sticks forward so far that it blocks the right eye's view of point A. When this happens, it is crucial that the pair of points given by using Equation (5.2) be colored differently, giving the eye a clue that hiding is happening. Naturally, we don't want to use some color so unusual that it violently clashes with the overall color scheme; if the stereogram is shades of blue and green, we don't want a bright red dot stuck into it. But the colors of points D and G must be clearly different from each other when one or both of their lines-of-sight are hidden by a nearer part of the object. If they are given the same color, as if no occlusion had occurred, the brain reacts badly, with the occluding part shimmering between being opaque and transparent, giving rise to an effect like a transporter malfunction on the *Enterprise*. It's not pleasant, and so it must be avoided.

The way we detect such occlusion is to follow the line-of-sight from point A toward the right eye. (Naturally, we also must do the same thing for the left eye, but we'll ignore that here because it is the same principle.) We shift to the right from the center column (that of point A) one column at a time. For each shifted column we compute the Z coordinate of the line-of-sight. If at any time we find an offset column whose Z value for the object is greater than or equal to that for the line-of-sight, we know that occlusion has occurred. The maximum possible value of Z on the object is 1, so we stop the search when we reach Z=1.

The small triangle defined by A–F–E is similar to the large triangle A–C–*RightEye*. Thus, the ratio shown in Equation (5.4) holds. From that, we solve for Z_k as shown in Equation (5.5).

$$\frac{k}{(Z_k - Z_0)\mu} = \frac{Eye/2}{(2 - \mu Z_0)} \tag{5.4}$$

$$Z_k = Z_0 + \left[\frac{2(2 - \mu Z_0)}{\mu\, Eye}\right] k \tag{5.5}$$

The Mapping Data Structure

The key data structure in the program is the Mapping. We keep an array of these to cover every possible color in a row of the stereogram. The *constraint class* of each pixel in the row points to an element of this array of Mapping elements. To help understand this, take a look back at Figure 2 on Page 9. Points *A*, *B*, and *C* are columns in a row of the stereogram. Because they are constrained to be identical, all three of these columns will be in the same constraint class, and this constraint class will be an index into the array of Mapping objects. The components of this Mapping object refer to the sprite pixel that determined the color that all of these constrained columns share.

It may be that the user has used the red channel of the depth image to define an area of focus. If not, the program makes the arbitrary choice of setting the focus to the center column of the image. The nearness member is the number of columns separating the focus column from the column whose (r,g,b) sprite color defines the color of this mapping. The idea is to keep the nearness as small as possible so that the defining color is that of the corresponding sprite column that is closest to the focus. We update the mapping every time nearness improves by dint of adding a constrained column whose corresponding sprite column is closer to the focus. This makes sure that the stereogram colors near the focus match to the greatest degree possible with the user's focus texture.

We also keep track of the Z (depth) of the column that determined this color. One thing to keep in mind is that the Z of some column far from the focus can be very different from the Z in its mapping, which is defined by the column in this constraint class closest to the focus, not by the column itself. If this is not clear now (it probably is not), it should become more clear when the code is presented. Just remember this basic idea: each pixel in the row belongs to a constraint class, which is an index into an array of Mapping objects. The Mapping object defines the color for this pixel, and it also contains important information about the sprite and depth pixels that determined this color.

```
struct Mapping {
    double Z ;
    int nearness ;
    unsigned char r ;
    unsigned char g ;
    unsigned char b ;
    } ;
```

The Code

We now plug through the code, focusing on key components. We begin with initialization. Here is that code, and a discussion follows on the next page.

```
focus = oversamp * nc / 2 ;          // Default if not specified for this row
for (icol=0 ; icol<oversamp*nc ; icol++) {
  constraint_class[icol] = -1 ;      // Flag unconstrained

  ibase = icol / oversamp ;
  ijump = icol % oversamp ;
  if (stereo_params.interpz)
    frac = (double) ijump / (double) oversamp ;
  else
    frac = 0.0 ;

  if (depth_bytes == 1) {
    if (ibase == nc - 1)  // The last column cannot interpolate because there is no 'next' column
      row_depth[icol] = depptr[ibase] / 255.0 ;
    else
      row_depth[icol] = (depptr[ibase] + frac * (depptr[ibase+1] - depptr[ibase])) / 255.0 ;
    }

  else if (depth_bytes == 3) {
    if (ibase == nc - 1)
      row_depth[icol] = (depptr[3*ibase] + depptr[3*ibase+1]) / (2.0 * 255.0) ;
    else {
      row_depth[icol]  = depptr[3*ibase+0] + frac * (depptr[3*(ibase+1)+0] - depptr[3*ibase+0]) ;
      row_depth[icol] += depptr[3*ibase+1] + frac * (depptr[3*(ibase+1)+1] - depptr[3*ibase+1]) ;
      row_depth[icol] /= 2.0 * 255.0 ;
      }
    if (depptr[3*ibase+2] >= 128)  // Red is focus
      focus = icol ;   // Might be trivially better to put focus in middle of range for oversampling
    }
  }

ncolors = 0 ;  // Counts colors in the colormap
```

One nice thing about stereogram computation is that it is strongly parallel, in that each row is independent of the other rows. Thus our presentation will be in terms of a single row, and multiple rows will be done in parallel as separate threads.

First, we must deal with the concept of *oversampling*. Much of the computation is, of necessity, done with integer arithmetic, handling each column of the image individually. But some computations, particularly those involving hidden pixels, benefit from higher resolution. So we provide the option of expanding each row into a number of columns that is an integer multiple of the actual number of columns, computing the stereogram from this much higher resolution image, and then averaging adjacent pixels to reduce the resolution to its original value. So most of the time when we see nc, the original number of columns in the image, it is multiplied by oversamp, the oversampling factor.

By default, we set the focus column to the center of the image, knowing that this may be overruled later. We then pass across the entire row, setting each column's constraint_class to −1 as a flag that it is not yet constrained (assigned to a Mapping).

Most of the time when we oversample we will want to interpolate the depth image. For example, suppose the depth goes from 0.4 to 0.5 from one column to the next column. If we oversample by 4, we would want the depths of the expanded columns to be 0.4, 0.425, 0.45, 0.475, 0.5, as opposed to 0.4, 0.4, 0.4, 0.4, 0.5. This facilitates more accurate hidden pixel computation by reducing or eliminating the 'staircase' effect shown in Figure 38 on Page 72.

Note that we generally should not interpolate sprite colors, because this could produce colors that do not exist in the sprite and perhaps lead to ugly results.

I won't explain the remainder of this initialization code line-by-line, because it is straightforward. I'll just point out that the user parameter interpz controls whether we interpolate. When we are at the last column we cannot interpolate because we don't have a 'next' depth to work toward. Finally, we have to handle 8-bit and 24-bit depths separately. Rcall that for 24-bit depth images the depth is the mean of the blue and green channels (which are always equal in *Stereo*), and the red channel is used to define the focus column.

We also initialize ncolors to 0. This is the number of Mapping entries that define colors in the current row of the stereogram. Note that these entries need not be unique. Certainly, colors can and often will be duplicated, and even the other members of this structure may be duplicated, although this would be rare.

We pass across this row, left-to-right, oversampling as requested. Despite this directionality, the algorithm is almost perfectly symmetric, and the few tiny violations of symmetry are rare and inconsequential. This symmetry is not only nice on a psychological level, but it also prevents the occasional peculiar results that plagued early asymmetric stereogram algorithms.

We use sprite_? to hold the color of the sprite pixel being processed. If the width of the sprite image is less than that of the depth image (which determines the width of the stereogram), we wrap around to the beginning of the sprite.

Doubling Equation (5.2) and rounding computes the distance between the left-eye and right-eye intersections with the viewplane, which we then split into left-of-center and right-of-center parts. These are points D and G, respectively, in Figure 59 on Page 105.

Some people randomly truncate for the left and right locations, or alternate according to row number. I believe that consistently truncating for the left eye is best. If you change the truncation rule here, be aware that you will also need to change it several places later in the program as well. Finally, we skip this column if either of the constrained points is outside the image.

```
for (icol=0 ; icol<oversamp*nc ; icol++) {              // For every column of depth and output
  if (sprite_bytes == 1)
    sprite_b = sprptr[(icol/oversamp)%sprite_nc] ;       // Left aligned, repeated
  else if (sprite_bytes == 3) {
    sprite_b = sprptr[3*((icol/oversamp)%sprite_nc)+0] ;  // Blue
    sprite_g = sprptr[3*((icol/oversamp)%sprite_nc)+1] ;  // Green
    sprite_r = sprptr[3*((icol/oversamp)%sprite_nc)+2] ;  // Red
    }

  z = row_depth[icol] ;
  idist = (int) ((1.0 - mu * z) / (2.0 - mu * z) * oversamp * eye + 0.5) ;  // Equation (5.2), doubled

  left = icol - idist / 2 ;         // Split the distance into left and right
  if (left < 0)                     // If left eye's view is outside the view
    continue ;                      // Nothing more to do

  right = left + idist ;            // This point will be constrained: same as left
  if (right >= oversamp * nc)       // If we are outside the image
    continue ;                      // Nothing more to do
```

Here we handle the issue of one (or occasionally both) of the constrained points being hidden by a part of the object that is closer to the eyes. Look back at Equation (5.5) on Page 106. When k=0 we are at the center point between the eyes, the point in the depth map being processed. This is Point *A* in Figure 59 on Page 105. So we initialize k to 1 and advance this column offset one column at a time, marching backwards along the left-eye and right-eye lines-of-sight. The multiplier in this equation is saved in factor. We can stop checking when zk reaches 1.0, because no depth can be greater than 1.

We have some small incentive to make the eye separation be an even number of columns, because then the factor is the same for both eyes, which simplifies this code. (If you don't understand that, consider the derivation of Equation (5.5), in which the integer division Eye/2 appears.) So you should enforce this innocuous restriction in the user interface. On the other hand, if the eye separation is odd and you still use this method, the errors will be tiny and almost certainly inconsequential.

```
k = 1 ;                                              // Check this far on each side of this point
factor = 2.0 * (2.0 - mu * z) / (mu * oversamp * eye) ;  // Slope of line
hidden = 0 ;
for (;;) {                                           // Loop until hidden status is determined
  zk = z + k * factor ;                              // Move along the line of sight
  if (zk >= 1.0)                                     // Upper limit, so it can't be hidden
    break ;
  if ((icol >= k)  &&  (row_depth[icol-k] >= zk)) {  // Left eye
    hidden = 1 ;                                     // If this neighbor pt is in front of line of sight
    break ;
    }
  if ((icol + k < oversamp * nc)  &&  (row_depth[icol+k] >= zk)) {
    hidden = 1 ;
    break ;
    }
  ++k ;                                              // Keep checking, moving further from point
  }

if (hidden)
  continue ;                                         // Skip over left-right constraining code
```

At this time we know that neither eye had Point A at column icol hidden from it. We now must constrain the stereogram pixels at columns left (point D) and right (point G) to be identical. There are four possibilities:

1)   The left point is already constrained, but the right point is still unconstrained. Set the constraint class of the right column to that of the left, and update that Mapping's nearness, Z, and color if column icol is closer to the focus than the current constraint.

2)   The right point, but not the left, is already constrained. Treat as above, reversing the roles of left and right. Superficially, it might seem as if this is an impossible situation, because we are moving left to right. But if the depth suddenly plunges, right will suddenly increase, jumping past the prior right. Then, if the depth suddenly increases, right will jump back to a lower value. So as icol moves smoothly from left to right, the constrained columns can jump back and forth wildly.

3)   Both points are already constrained, so we have to combine the two constraint classes. Pass through the entire row, changing all occurrences of the right pixel's constraint class to that of the left. This implies a tiny, insignificant asymmetry when the left and right constraint classes are exactly the same distance from the focus. If they are different distances from the focus, the color map is updated to whichever is closer, resulting in symmetric behavior. Finally, update that Mapping's nearness, Z, and color if column icol is closer to the focus than the current constraint.

4)   Neither point is constrained. Add a new colormap Mapping entry with the information for column icol and set the constraint class of left and right to this new entry.

We handle case 3 first, the situation of both being constrained.

```
ccl = constraint_class[left] ;          // Class of pixel seen by left eye
ccr = constraint_class[right] ;         // And right

if (ccl >= 0) {                         // Is left constrained already?
  if (ccr >= 0) {                       // Is right constrained already?
    for (i=0 ; i<oversamp*nc ; i++) {   // For entire row
      if (constraint_class[i] == ccr)   // All pixels previously
        constraint_class[i] = ccl ;     // mapped to r's become l's
    } // For i, remapping constraint_class of right to left
```

```
    if (colormap[ccr].nearness == colormap[ccl].nearness) {        // Rare case of a tie for focus
      // This is where we can (likely pointlessly) ensure perfect symmetry
      // These next four lines are more philosophical than practical,
      // extreme overkill to force more symmetry for no good reason.
      if (abs(right-oversamp*nc/2) == abs(left-oversamp*nc/2))        // Also tied for nearness to center of image
        i = i ;  // Optionally do some sort of tie breaking here  (This condition is extremely rare and not a problem)
      else if (abs(right-oversamp*nc/2) < abs(left-oversamp*nc/2))    // Favor whichever is closer to center of image
        colormap[ccl] = colormap[ccr] ;
      }
    else if (colormap[ccr].nearness < colormap[ccl].nearness)        // Better? (unlike above, this test is vital)
      colormap[ccl] = colormap[ccr] ; // If so, get r's for l

    // Is this column best of all?
    if (abs(focus-icol) < colormap[ccl].nearness) {
      colormap[ccl].nearness = abs(focus-icol) ;
      colormap[ccl].Z = row_depth[icol] ;
      colormap[ccl].b = sprite_b ;
      if (sprite_bytes == 3) {
        colormap[ccl].g = sprite_g ;
        colormap[ccl].r = sprite_r ;
        }
      }

    } // Left and right are both constrained, so absorb r into l
```

After remapping all columns, we compare the quality (nearness to focus) of the two color maps that were just merged. The important action is to change the left (absorbing) color map to the right (absorbed) if the right is closer to the focus. This is handled in the 'else if' line. That big 'if' at the beginning is pretty much unnecessary, as it just handles the rare case of a tie for nearness, in which case it really doesn't matter what we do. But to get a warm, fuzzy feeling, I made a small attempt to break the tie in order to ensure better symmetry. There's really no practical reason to go to this extreme, but it's harmless and it feels good.

It may be that the column that triggered this merging of two constraint classes is closer to the focus than either of the two merged classes. When this happens, we update the color map to reflect this 'best of all' column.

The next two code blocks handle the first and second cases. All we do is set the unconstrained column's color map to that of the constrained column and then update the color map if this triggering column is closer to the focus.

```
else {  // Left is constrained, but right is not

  constraint_class[right] = ccl ;

  if (abs(focus-icol) < colormap[ccl].nearness) {
    colormap[ccl].nearness = abs(focus-icol) ;
    colormap[ccl].Z = row_depth[icol] ;
    colormap[ccl].b = sprite_b ;
    if (sprite_bytes == 3) {
      colormap[ccl].g = sprite_g ;
      colormap[ccl].r = sprite_r ;
      }
    }
  }   // Left is constrained, but right is not
} // If left is constrained

else {  // Left is not already constrained

  if (ccr >= 0) {  // Right constrained already?

    constraint_class[left] = ccr ;

    if (abs(focus-icol) < colormap[ccr].nearness){
      colormap[ccr].nearness = abs(focus-icol) ;
      colormap[ccr].Z = row_depth[icol] ;
      colormap[ccr].b = sprite_b ;
      if (sprite_bytes == 3) {
        colormap[ccr].g = sprite_g ;
        colormap[ccr].r = sprite_r ;
        }
      }
    } // Left is not constrained, but right is
```

Last of all, we handle the fourth case: neither the left nor the right columns are constrained yet. Constrain them both to this column's color.

```
      else { // Neither is constrained yet.  Do it now.

        constraint_class[right] = constraint_class[left] = ncolors ;
        colormap[ncolors].nearness = abs(focus-icol) ;
        colormap[ncolors].Z = row_depth[icol] ;
        colormap[ncolors].b = sprite_b ;
        if (sprite_bytes == 3) {
          colormap[ncolors].g = sprite_g ;
          colormap[ncolors].r = sprite_r ;
          }
        ++ncolors ;
        }
      } // Left is not already constrained
    } // For all columns, computing constraints
```

We have finished the core computation of the stereogram for all columns of this row. But there are two more issues to deal with. The first, which we now explore, is an optional algorithm that sometimes helps significantly with improving the appearance of a stereogram that is plagued by numerous hidden pixels due to rapid depth changes. It also sometimes harms appearance, so it is made a user option.

We loop through the columns that surround the focus, which comprise the most important columns. As we did earlier, we compute the left and right constrained columns and skip processing if either is outside the image.

```
  if (stereo_params.hidfix) {

    for (icol=focus-oversamp*eye/2 ; icol<=focus+oversamp*eye/2 ; icol++) {
      if (icol < 0  ||  icol >= oversamp*nc)
        continue ;

      z = row_depth[icol] ;
      idist = (int) ((1.0 - mu * z) / (2.0 - mu * z) * oversamp * eye + 0.5) ;
```

```
left = icol - idist / 2 ;   // Split the distance into left and right
if (left < 0)               // If left eye's view is outside the view
  continue ;                // Nothing more to do

right = left + idist ;      // This point will be constrained: same as left
if (right >= oversamp * nc) // If we are outside the image
  continue ;                // Nothing more to do
```

We now repeat the same hidden-pixel algorithm that we used before, although this time we discriminate according to which eye's view is obstructed. This algorithm is the dominant time-eater in the program, so a more efficient approach would be to compute this vector once and then reuse it, rather than computing it twice. But it's more clear this way, not used very often, and fast on modern computers, so I did it this way. If neither point is hidden, we have nothing to do here.

```
left_hidden = right_hidden = 0 ;
k = 1 ;                                              // Check this far on each side of this point
factor = 2.0 * (2.0 - mu * z) / (mu * oversamp * eye) ;   // Slope of line
for (;;) {                                           // Loop until hidden status is determined

  zk = z + k * factor ;                              // Move along the line of sight
  if (zk >= 1.0)                                     // Upper limit, so it can't be hidden
    break ;

  if ((icol >= k)  &&  (row_depth[icol-k] >= zk)) {  // Left eye
    left_hidden = icol-k ;                           // If this neighbor pt is in front of line of sight
    assert ( left_hidden > 0 ) ;                     // Should always be true, but be sure
    }

  if ((icol + k < oversamp * nc)  &&  (row_depth[icol+k] >= zk)) {
    right_hidden = icol+k ;
    assert ( right_hidden < oversamp * nc ) ;
    }

  ++k ;         // Keep checking, moving further from point
  }

if (! left_hidden  &&  ! right_hidden)
  continue ;
```

We now handle (separately for left and right) the situation of exactly one eye being shadowed. Let k be the constraint class of the non-hidden point on the stereogram viewplane, and in case it is not yet constrained we give it a fresh class, setting its Z to ensure that the next 'if' block executes. Because one point is hidden, the prior algorithm refrained from constraining the two points to be the same color, which would ultimately cause them to be set more or less randomly later. (Either of these columns may already be constrained to some *other* column from a different triggering column.) Here we see if the triggering column icol has a depth that is closer to the observer than the depth of the triggering column that determined the color of this non-hidden side. If so, we change the color map of the non-hidden column to be the color of icol. This almost certainly will not violate the rule that says these two columns must be different colors, but it will make the color of this non-hidden column more 'sensible' by setting it to what that eye would see.

```
if (right_hidden  && ! left_hidden) {
  k = constraint_class[left] ;
  if (k < 0) {
    k = constraint_class[left] = ncolors ;
    colormap[ncolors].Z = -1 ;
    ++ncolors ;
    }
  if (colormap[k].Z < row_depth[icol]) {
    colormap[k].r = sprptr[3*((icol/oversamp)%sprite_nc)+2] ;
    colormap[k].g = sprptr[3*((icol/oversamp)%sprite_nc)+1] ;
    colormap[k].b = sprptr[3*((icol/oversamp)%sprite_nc)+0] ;
    colormap[k].nearness = abs(icol-focus) ;
    colormap[k].Z = row_depth[icol] ;
    }
  }

if (left_hidden  && ! right_hidden) {
  ... Do what we did above, but with left-right roles reversed...
  }

  } // For icol, post-processing hidden
} // Hid fix
```

We now perform one more 'fixing' operation. This algorithm never causes problems (at least as far as I've seen), and it very often significantly, almost miraculously, improves the stereogram. Thus, it is not optional.

Recall that we scan across the depth image one column at a time. For each depth column, we compute a pair of columns (left and right) in the stereogram that must be constrained to be the same color. But if there was a discontinuity in depth, some columns can be skipped on the left, the right, or both. These skipped columns remain at whatever they were before, which may be unconstrained, or more likely, constrained to some inappropriate color. Regardless, the sudden contrasting color looks awful if it's in the middle of an important focus region.

For example, suppose the depth suddenly takes a nosedive as you are moving left-to-right. The distance between the left and right constrained points suddenly jumps up. So the sequence of 'right' columns may be 125, 126, 127, 130... with 128 and 129 in the viewplane skipped at the large depth discontinuity. If you do not have a focus region here, this makes no difference; it just ends up being some part of the sprite and nearly always looks fine. But suppose columns 127 and 130 are (correctly) part of a red area in the focus texture. If 128 and 129 are just set to some more-or-less random color instead of red, it looks terrible. So we fill in the skipped gap with something appropriate.

The solution is to scan all columns and do the same left/right calculation we did originally. If we have two adjacent depth columns that produce a left or right gap in the stereogram, we must change the colormap information for those otherwise undefined columns inside the gap.

If an interior skipped column is already constrained, the most common situation, we have to leave these constraints alone and just update this constraint class's color map. (The only reason either left or right is still unconstrained (constraint_class == –1) is if it was a victim of hidden pixel elimination or the other side was past the image edge.)

There are several rules that help us find a good new color for these interior gaps:

1) Preference should be given to skipped columns that come from sprite columns that are nearest to the focus. Thus, we start at the focus and check successively further adjacent pairs, first to the left of focus, then to the right. When we update a color map, we set its nearness=–1 as a flag that it has been updated. Do not then set any that are already set (nearness=–1). This favors sprite columns near the focus.

2)   Rapidly changing colors give an unpleasant sparkly appearance to the image, so we should pick the color at one end of the gap and reproduce it throughout the gap.

3)   Which end do we pick to define the interior color? The end with greater Z (nearer the eyes) may hide the other end, so it is the more sensible choice.

4)   In case the Zs are tied, we choose whichever column in the pair is closer to the focus (inner).

5)   It's probably good to avoid setting interior points when the gap exceeds one column in the original (pre-oversampling) scale. This minimizes huge, ugly errors that can occur, although at the expense of leaving some unfixed gaps when oversampling is too small. But by increasing oversamp enough we can always satisfy this because when we raise oversamp, we also decrease Z jumps, and it does not take a lot of oversampling for idist to drop under oversamp.

6)   If both endpoints have the same color, there's no harm in setting all interior points to this color. This would be rare in most situations, but a no-brainer when it happens.

This gap-filling remapping is done 4 times in the code:
    Left of focus
       Left idist/2
       Right idist/2
    Right of focus
       Left idist/2
       Right idist/2

I'll show only the first of these four instances here; the other three are identical in effect, just with different boundaries. These four instances occur inside an outer loop that begins with focus_dist=1, a distance of just one column from the focus, and the loop continues for as long as there are still columns on either side of the focus. This is shown in the block of code on the next page. The 'if' is the condition that there is still at least one column on the left side of the focus. We'll want to compute left and right constrained columns for this column (the 'outer' because it is further from the focus) as well as the column on its right (the 'inner').

```
for (focus_dist=1 ; (focus-focus_dist>=0) || (focus+focus_dist<oversamp*nc) ; focus_dist++) {

  if (focus - focus_dist >= 0) {

    // Left column in this adjacent pair
    icol = focus-focus_dist ;        // Outer (further from focus) of a pair of adjacent sprite/depth columns
    z = row_depth[icol] ;
    idist = (int) ((1.0 - mu * z) / (2.0 - mu * z) * oversamp * eye + 0.5) ;
    outerL = icol - idist / 2 ;       // These are the columns originally used for constraining
    outerR = outerL + idist ;

    // Right column in this adjacent pair
    icol = icol+1 ;                   // Inner (closer to focus) of a pair of adjacent sprite/depth columns
    z = row_depth[icol] ;
    idist = (int) ((1.0 - mu * z) / (2.0 - mu * z) * oversamp * eye + 0.5) ;
    innerL = icol - idist / 2 ;       // These are the columns originally used for constraining
    innerR = innerL + idist ;
```

We now process the left constrained columns for each of these adjacent sprite/depth columns. The depth may have jumped up or down for the adjacent columns, so their 'left' columns may have skipped up or down; we don't know which. Also, we must bound them at the leftmost column of the stereogram. So do this bounding and put them in order. The skipped columns are inside the computed left points, so we add/subtract 1 to get the first and last skipped columns.

```
    outerL = (outerL >= 0) ? outerL : 0 ;    // Bound at left side of stereogram
    innerL = (innerL >= 0) ? innerL : 0 ;

    if (outerL < innerL) {            // Put them in increasing order
      istart = outerL + 1 ;           // These are the skipped columns now subject to revision
      istop = innerL - 1 ;            // First and last
    }
    else {
      istart = innerL + 1 ;
      istop = outerL - 1 ;
    }

    cc_outer = constraint_class[outerL] ;    // Constraint class of endpoint
    cc_inner = constraint_class[innerL] ;
```

We'll use ok_to_postproc as a flag to signal whether this segment should be processed. The condition istop>=istart says that there is a gap of at least one skipped column. We also need both endpoints to be constrained to some color, as opposed to having been the victim of being hidden or one of the left-right pair being outside the image. If any of these three conditions fail, we have nothing useful to do.

If these basic conditions are met, we look at a situation that is important to visual appearance, especially in 'normal' vision as opposed to 3D vision. If the number of columns in the gap is more than one column in the original image, we would be setting a contiguous block of columns to the same color, which looks strange. (See rule 5 a few pages ago. Note that setting the limit at 1 column is arbitrary, and could just as well be 2 or more, although even 2 identical columns often looks funny.) On first consideration, this restriction would seem to be counterproductive, as we would refrain from doing this vitally important color revision just when we need it the most! But as long as we interpolate the depth when oversampling, as discussed as the beginning of this section, we can always find an oversampling rate sufficiently large that this condition never causes a problem. So this is not really an impediment to the algorithm, and it is a valuable check on overly enthusiastic color revision.

Finally, we take care of a fairly unusual but easy situation. If both endpoints are the same color, then it is almost certainly fine to make the interior that same color. Of course, it is theoretically possible for this to be excessive confidence, but it is extremely rare; I've never seen it cause a problem.

Some readers may wish to increase that limit of 1 in the gap check, to 2 or perhaps even 3, or make it a user parameter. Also, some readers may want to eliminate the 'both ends same color' test, or make it optional. Feel free. I like things the way they are.

```
ok_to_postproc = 0 ;
if (istop >= istart  &&  cc_outer >= 0  &&  cc_inner >= 0) {  // This is the basic constraint
  ok_to_postproc = 1 ;
  if (istop - istart + 1 > oversamp)       // Prevent occasional huge ugly blotches
    ok_to_postproc = 0 ;                   // Sufficient oversampling will make this always false

  if (colormap[cc_outer].r == colormap[cc_inner].r &&  // This is a no-brainer
    colormap[cc_outer].g == colormap[cc_inner].g &&
    colormap[cc_outer].b == colormap[cc_inner].b)
    ok_to_postproc = 1 ;
  }
```

At this point, we know we are going to remap the interior points, previously skipped over due to a rapid depth change. But which end shall we use to determine the new color? Rules 3 and 4 presented a few pages ago tell us the answer: we favor whichever end is closer to the observer (greater depth). In case the depth is tied, we favor whichever is closer to the focus. This happens automatically if we include equality, because the inner column, by how it is defined, is closer to the focus than the outer column.

Finally, we loop through every gap column. In the fairly unusual case that it is not yet constrained, we create a new constraint class for it. We set its nearness to any positive number so it passes the revision test a few lines later. If it has not yet been changed (recall that we are working from closest to focus toward more distance) then reset its color and Z to the endpoint's values, and set its nearness to -1 so it is not changed again.

```
if (ok_to_postproc) {
    if (colormap[cc_inner].Z >= colormap[cc_outer].Z) // We include equal to favor inner if Z tied
        cc_copied = cc_inner ;
    else
        cc_copied = cc_outer ;

    for (icol=istart ; icol<=istop ; icol++) {
        if (constraint_class[icol] < 0) {                           // Still unconstrained? (fairly unusual)
            constraint_class[icol] = ncolors++ ;                    // Give it its own new constraint class
            colormap[constraint_class[icol]].nearness = 99999999 ;  // Anything not negative
        }

        k = constraint_class[icol] ;

        if (colormap[k].nearness < 0)
            continue ;

        colormap[k].r = colormap[cc_copied].r ;
        colormap[k].g = colormap[cc_copied].g ;
        colormap[k].b = colormap[cc_copied].b ;
        colormap[k].Z = colormap[cc_copied].Z ;
        colormap[k].nearness = -1 ;   // Do not let this column be updated again, as we favor close to focus.
    }
} // Left of focus, left gap
```

There are still a few things left to do to complete the stereogram, but they are all straightforward so I won't bother reproducing the code here. The complete source code is in M3D_1.CPP. Nonetheless, a few thoughts are in order.

- When we assign a color to each column, if the column is constrained (which is nearly always the case), we just copy the RBG entries from the Mapping color map. For those rare columns that are unconstrained, there is no mandatory color to use, and different people use different rules. My choice is to use the sprite pixel that is offset from the column by one-quarter of the eye separation. I have found that this choice usually looks fine because it is taken directly from the background sprite and so does not stand out as weird. Moreover, it is less likely than other choices to create funny artifacts if there are blocks of unconstrained columns.

- If oversampling has been done, I compute the final stereogram color as the average of the oversampled values, doing each band separately. This, of course, can theoretically create stereogram colors that do not exist in the sprite, which some people find disagreeable (though I do not). Using a median instead of an average reduces the degree to which this happens, at a price of enormously more computing time if the oversampling is large.

- Column medians, if requested by the user, can be computed as each row is done, but row medians are most easily computed after the entire stereogram has been computed. In most cases I can see no difference with and without median filtering, but in some noisy situations it can make a small but noticeable improvement.

- The source code file M3D_1.CPP includes all of my thread launching code. I'm not going to take the time here to walk through it, because many readers will just keep things simple by using a single thread, while others may make use of Microsoft's built-in threading framework, which I do not. Moreover, the code is well commented, so additional explanation should not be needed. Readers who desire a detailed walkthrough of my method of multithreading can find it in all three of my Deep Belief Net books, as well as my Data Mining book.

- In any stereogram program, it's nice to include an option of printing eye-convergence blocks to aid inexperienced viewers. This was discussed on Page 10. Printing these blocks is the last action taken by the code.

6

The Single-Object Stereogram Algorithm

The geometry and key equations for the single-object texture-mapped stereogram are almost identical to what we saw for sprite-based stereograms, so we'll dispense with the introductory material. Please be familiar with the prior chapter in its entirety before proceeding on to this chapter, as I'll be doing abbreviated discussions of material that was covered in the prior chapter. Complete code is in M3D_2.CPP.

The Mapping structure is similar to that for the sprite version, but it is different in two ways. First, there is no focus column in a texture-mapped stereogram; the texture itself is the 'focus' that we favor. Thus, there is no nearness member. In its place we have the is_texture flag. If this pixel is background, this flag will be 0. Ordinary texture will be indicated by a value of 1, and red 'super-texture' (Page 54) with 2. Because we have the (default and normally used) option of averaging texture when instances overlap, we need the n_texture member to count how many textures have gone into the average so far.

```
struct Mapping {
    double Z ;         // Z of whatever gave best color (or max of Zs if texture ties)
    int is_texture ;   // 0=background; 1=ordinary texture; 2= red-depth super-texture
    int n_texture ;    // Number of texture colors that went into this color (used only if ! favor_Z)
    unsigned char r ;
    unsigned char g ;
    unsigned char b ;
    } ;
```

The calling parameter list is essentially identical to that for the sprite-based method:

```
static void make_3d_2_worker (
    int irow ,                    // Not used for algorithm; for debugging only
    int nc ,                      // Number of columns in depth and output images
    int texture_bytes ,           // Bytes-per-pixel in texture and output (1 or 3)
    int depth_bytes ,             // Bytes-per-pixel in depth (1 or 3)
    unsigned char *txtptr ,       // Input single row in texture image
    unsigned char *depptr ,       // Input single row in depth image
    unsigned char *rowptr ,       // Output single row of stereo image
    int oversamp ,                // Oversampling rate
    int *constraint_class ,       // Work array oversamp * nc long
    Mapping *colormap ,           // Work array oversamp * nc long
    double *row_depth ,           // Work array oversamp * nc long
    unsigned char *row_work       // Work array oversamp * nc * sprite_bytes long
    )
```

Fetch a few parameters and options that are global. You could just as well pass these as parameters to avoid global references. Also, we define the color that will indicate background in the texture map. Everywhere else in the Stereo program the background is defined by pure black, but here we allow an arbitrary definition.

```
eye = stereo_params.eye_spacing ;          // These could be passed as parameters to avoid global reference
mu = stereo_params.mu ;
favor_Z = stereo_params.favor_Z ;          // Favor Z when instances overlap (vs averaginging)
honor_red = stereo_params.honor_red ;      // Use super-texture as defined by the red channel of depth?
bg_r = bg_g = bg_b = (unsigned char) 0 ;   // Defined background color
```

Initialization is the same as in the sprite version, except that we do not have to worry about a focus column:

```
for (icol=0 ; icol<oversamp*nc ; icol++) {
  constraint_class[icol] = -1 ;  // Flag unconstrained
  ibase = icol / oversamp ;
  ijump = icol % oversamp ;
  if (stereo_params.interpz)
    frac = (double) ijump / (double) oversamp ;
  else
    frac = 0.0 ;
  if (depth_bytes == 1) {
    if (ibase == nc - 1)   // The last column cannot interpolate because there is no 'next' column
      row_depth[icol] = depptr[ibase] / 255.0 ;
    else
      row_depth[icol] = (depptr[ibase] + frac * (depptr[ibase+1] - depptr[ibase])) / 255.0 ;
    }
  else if (depth_bytes == 3) {
    if (ibase == nc - 1)
      row_depth[icol] = (depptr[3*ibase] + depptr[3*ibase+1]) / (2.0 * 255.0) ;
    else {
      row_depth[icol]  = depptr[3*ibase+0] + frac * (depptr[3*(ibase+1)+0] - depptr[3*ibase+0]) ;
      row_depth[icol] += depptr[3*ibase+1] + frac * (depptr[3*(ibase+1)+1] - depptr[3*ibase+1]) ;
      row_depth[icol] /= 2.0 * 255.0 ;
      }
    }
  }
ncolors = 0 ;  // Counts colors in the colormap
```

As in the sprite version, we loop across columns of this row, letting texture_? be the color of the current texture pixel. Compute the left and right constrained columns, and skip processing if either is outside the image.

```
for (icol=0 ; icol<oversamp*nc ; icol++) {          // For every column of this row
  if (texture_bytes == 1)
    texture_b = txtptr[icol/oversamp] ;
  else if (texture_bytes == 3) {
    texture_b = txtptr[3*(icol/oversamp)+0] ;        // Blue
    texture_g = txtptr[3*(icol/oversamp)+1] ;        // Green
    texture_r = txtptr[3*(icol/oversamp)+2] ;        // Red
    }

  z = row_depth[icol] ;
  idist = (int) ((1.0 - mu * z) / (2.0 - mu * z) * oversamp * eye + 0.5) ;

  left = icol - idist / 2 ;          // Split the distance into left and right
  if (left < 0)                      // If left eye's view is outside the view
    continue ;                       // Nothing more to do

  right = left + idist ;             // This point will be constrained: same as left
  if (right >= oversamp * nc)        // If we are outside the image
    continue ;                       // Nothing more to do
```

We check to see if this column is hidden by a part of the object closer to the observer, exactly as we did in the sprite version:

```
  k = 1 ;                   // Check this far on each side of this point
  factor = 2.0 * (2.0 - mu * z) / (mu * oversamp * eye) ; // Slope of line
  hidden = 0 ;
  for (;;) {                // Loop until hidden status is determined
    zk = z + k * factor ;   // Move along the line of sight
    if (zk >= 1.0)          // Upper limit, so it can't be hidden
      break ;
    if ((icol >= k)  &&  (row_depth[icol-k] >= zk)) { // Left eye
      hidden = 1 ;          // If this neighbor pt is in front of line of sight
      break ;
      }
```

```
if ((icol + k < oversamp * nc)  &&  (row_depth[icol+k] >= zk)) {
  hidden = 1 ;
  break ;
  }
++k ;          // Keep checking, moving further from point
}
```

Once we know that this column is not hidden, we check the same four possibilities that we had in the sprite version. But here is where things get more complicated. In the sprite version, there was no such concept as a background that was to be ignored. Every pixel played a role. But in the texture-mapped version we ignore columns that are part of the background. Moreover, if instances overlap we have to deal with either favoring the closer instance or averaging colors (which is usually superior). Let's begin with the 'both are constrained' situation, noting that the initial remapping is the same as in the sprite version.

```
ccl = constraint_class[left] ;         // Class of pixel seen by left eye
ccr = constraint_class[right] ;        // And right

if (ccl >= 0) {                        // Is left constrained already?
  if (ccr >= 0) {                      // Right constrained already?
    for (i=0 ; i<oversamp*nc ; i++) {
      if (constraint_class[i] == ccr)  // All pixels previously
        constraint_class[i] = ccl ;    // mapped to r's become l's
    } // For i, remapping constraint_class of right to left
```

The next 'if' statement handles the complex situation of instance overlap. Its 'else if' clause is straightforward: if the absorbed class is texture but the absorbing class is background (not texture), make the new, combined color map be that of the texture. That was easy. But now let's consider the situation of both of these merged constraint classes being texture, which happens when the texture is so wide that instances overlap. Now we have three possibilities:

1) The user has requested that we honor the red channel of the depth image as a super-texture flag, and the absorbed class is super-texture. Make the combined class be that texture.

2) The absorbing class is not super-texture and the user has not requested favoring Z. Compute the new color as a weighted average of the merged colors and update the counter for any subsequent weighting.

3) The absorbing class is not super-texture and the user wants to favor Z. If the absorbed class is closer to the observer than the absorbing class, let the absorbed class's color determine the merged class's color.

```
if (colormap[ccr].is_texture && colormap[ccl].is_texture) {        // Overlap case of both being texture
  if (colormap[ccr].is_texture == 2)                                // Super-texture?
    colormap[ccl] = colormap[ccr] ;
  else if (colormap[ccl].is_texture != 2  &&  ! favor_Z) {
    colormap[ccl].Z = (colormap[ccr].Z > colormap[ccl].Z) ? colormap[ccr].Z : colormap[ccl].Z ;
    colormap[ccl].b = (unsigned char) ((colormap[ccl].n_texture * colormap[ccl].b +
                                 colormap[ccr].n_texture * colormap[ccr].b) /
                                 (double) (colormap[ccl].n_texture + colormap[ccr].n_texture)) ;
    colormap[ccl].g = (unsigned char) ((colormap[ccl].n_texture * colormap[ccl].g +
                                 colormap[ccr].n_texture * colormap[ccr].g) /
                                 (double) (colormap[ccl].n_texture + colormap[ccr].n_texture)) ;
    colormap[ccl].r = (unsigned char) ((colormap[ccl].n_texture * colormap[ccl].r +
                                 colormap[ccr].n_texture * colormap[ccr].r) /
                                 (double) (colormap[ccl].n_texture + colormap[ccr].n_texture)) ;
    colormap[ccl].n_texture += colormap[ccr].n_texture ;
    }
  else if (colormap[ccl].is_texture != 2  &&   colormap[ccr].Z > colormap[ccl].Z)   // Favor whichever is closer to viewer
    colormap[ccl] = colormap[ccr] ;
  }

else if (colormap[ccr].is_texture  &&  ! colormap[ccl].is_texture)  // Better?
  colormap[ccl] = colormap[ccr] ; // If so, get r's for l
```

Just as we did for the sprite version, we have to see if this column is the best of all. In the sprite version, we defined superiority as being closer to the focus column. Here it's more complicated. First of all, this column can only be in the running for 'best' if it is texture, so we don't bother checking for superiority if it is background. If it is texture, there are three possibilities:

1) The user has requested that we honor the red channel of the depth image as super-texture, and this column is super-texture. We reset everything to this pixel. The color map gets this pixel's color and depth, the texture count becomes 1 (this pixel alone set the color), and we flag that this column is super-texture.

2) The existing class is also texture and the user does not want to favor Z. If the merged class is not super-texture, compute a weighted average of the existing color and this pixel, and update the texture counter to account for this pixel.

3) Otherwise, if the merged class is not super-texture and the current column is closer, or if the merged class is background, reset as we did in the first case, but flag that this is ordinary texture.

```
if (texture_r != bg_r  ||  texture_g != bg_g  ||  texture_b != bg_b) {          // Is this column texture?

   if (honor_red  &&  depptr[3*(icol/oversamp)+2] >= 128) {          // Is it super-texture?
      colormap[ccl].n_texture = 1 ;
      colormap[ccl].is_texture = 2 ;
      colormap[ccl].Z = row_depth[icol] ;
      colormap[ccl].b = texture_b ;
      colormap[ccl].g = texture_g ;
      colormap[ccl].r = texture_r ;
      }

   else if (colormap[ccl].is_texture  && ! favor_Z) {  // Most common if texture wider than rep width for this Z
      if (colormap[ccl].is_texture != 2) {
         colormap[ccl].Z = (row_depth[icol] > colormap[ccl].Z) ? row_depth[icol] : colormap[ccl].Z ;
         colormap[ccl].b = (unsigned char) ((colormap[ccl].n_texture * colormap[ccl].b + texture_b) /
                     (colormap[ccl].n_texture + 1.0)) ;
         colormap[ccl].g = (unsigned char) ((colormap[ccl].n_texture * colormap[ccl].g + texture_g) /
                     (colormap[ccl].n_texture + 1.0)) ;
         colormap[ccl].r = (unsigned char) ((colormap[ccl].n_texture * colormap[ccl].r + texture_r) /
                     (colormap[ccl].n_texture + 1.0)) ;
         ++colormap[ccl].n_texture ;
         }
      }

   // Closer or ccl not texture?
   else if ((colormap[ccl].is_texture != 2 && row_depth[icol] > colormap[ccl].Z)  || ! colormap[ccl].is_texture) {
      colormap[ccl].n_texture = 1 ;
      colormap[ccl].is_texture = 1 ;
      colormap[ccl].Z = row_depth[icol] ;
      colormap[ccl].b = texture_b ;
      colormap[ccl].g = texture_g ;
      colormap[ccl].r = texture_r ;
      }
   }

} // Left and right are both constrained, so absorb r into l
```

There's no point in wasting paper to show the cases of one or the other being constrained. All we do is set the constraint class of the unconstrained to that of the constrained and then handle the situation of the current column being best of all, exactly as we did in the code just shown for the 'both constrained' situation.

The fourth possibility is that neither the left nor the right are constrained. Create a new Mapping for this new constraint class. Set its is_texture flag according to whether it is background, texture, or super-texture. Set the texture counter to 1, because this is the sole color so far, and copy this column's depth and colors.

```
          constraint_class[right] = constraint_class[left] = ncolors ;
          colormap[ncolors].is_texture = texture_r != bg_r || texture_g != bg_g || texture_b != bg_b ;
          if (honor_red && colormap[ncolors].is_texture && depptr[3*(icol/oversamp)+2] >= 128)   // Is it super-texture?
            colormap[ncolors].is_texture = 2 ;
          colormap[ncolors].n_texture = colormap[ncolors].is_texture ? 1 : 0 ;
          colormap[ncolors].Z = row_depth[icol] ;
          colormap[ncolors].b = texture_b ;
          colormap[ncolors].g = texture_g ;
          colormap[ncolors].r = texture_r ;
          ++ncolors ;
          }
        } // Left is not already constrained
      } // For all columns, computing constraints
```

We now handle the user option of attempting to fix hidden-pixel problems. In the sprite version we worked around the focus, but there is no focus for texture-mapped stereograms; the texture itself is the focus. So we just loop across all columns, and check for problems only at texture columns. The hidden-pixel algorithm is exactly the same as in the sprite version.

```
  if (stereo_params.hidfix) {

    for (icol=0 ; icol<oversamp*nc ; icol++) {

      // If this column is background, nothing to do ;
      if (txtptr[3*(icol/oversamp)+0] == bg_b && txtptr[3*(icol/oversamp)+1] == bg_g && txtptr[3*(icol/oversamp)+2] == bg_r)
        continue ;

      z = row_depth[icol] ;
      idist = (int) ((1.0 - mu * z) / (2.0 - mu * z) * oversamp * eye + 0.5) ;
```

```
left = icol - idist / 2 ;          // Split the distance into left and right
if (left < 0)                      // If left eye's view is outside the view
  continue ;                       // Nothing more to do

right = left + idist ;             // This point will be constrained: same as left
if (right >= oversamp * nc)        // If we are outside the image
  continue ;                       // Nothing more to do

left_hidden = right_hidden = 0 ;
k = 1 ;                            // Check this far on each side of this point
factor = 2.0 * (2.0 - mu * z) / (mu * oversamp * eye) ; // Slope of line
for (;;) {                         // Loop until hidden status is determined
  zk = z + k * factor ;            // Move along the line of sight
  if (zk >= 1.0)                   // Upper limit, so it can't be hidden
    break ;
  if ((icol >= k)  &&  (row_depth[icol-k] >= zk)) { // One eye
    left_hidden = icol-k ;         // If this neighbor pt is in front of line of sight
    assert ( left_hidden > 0 ) ;
    }
  if ((icol + k < oversamp * nc)  &&  (row_depth[icol+k] >= zk)) {
    right_hidden = icol+k ;
    assert ( right_hidden < oversamp * nc ) ;
    }
  ++k ;                            // Keep checking, moving further from point
  }

if (! left_hidden  &&  ! right_hidden) // If this column is not hidden from either eye, nothing to do
  continue ;
```

When we get here, we know that at least one eye is obscured. The fixing algorithm is essentially identical to that for the sprite version, so please refer back to that for details. The only difference is that instead of setting a nearness member, we set the is_texture member. We don't need to set n_texture because we are all done with that.

```
// ---> Hidden from right eye only

if (right_hidden  &&  ! left_hidden) {
  k = constraint_class[left] ;
  if (k < 0) {
    k = constraint_class[left] = ncolors ;
    colormap[ncolors].Z = -1 ;
    ++ncolors ;
  }
  if (colormap[k].Z < row_depth[icol]) {
    colormap[k].r = txtptr[3*(icol/oversamp)+2] ;
    colormap[k].g = txtptr[3*(icol/oversamp)+1] ;
    colormap[k].b = txtptr[3*(icol/oversamp)+0] ;
    colormap[k].is_texture = 1 ;
    colormap[k].Z = row_depth[icol] ;
  }
  } // if (right_hidden  &&  ! left_hidden)


// ---> Hidden from left eye only

if (left_hidden  &&  ! right_hidden) {
  k = constraint_class[right] ;
  if (k < 0) {
    k = constraint_class[right] = ncolors ;
    colormap[ncolors].Z = -1 ;
    ++ncolors ;
  }
  if (colormap[k].Z < row_depth[icol]) {
    colormap[k].r = txtptr[3*(icol/oversamp)+2] ;
    colormap[k].g = txtptr[3*(icol/oversamp)+1] ;
    colormap[k].b = txtptr[3*(icol/oversamp)+0] ;
    colormap[k].is_texture = 1 ;
    colormap[k].Z = row_depth[icol] ;
  }
  }
  } // For icol, post-processing hidden
} // Hid fix
```

The algorithm for fixing skipped columns operates on the same general principle as that in the sprite version, but the exact steps are somewhat different because we are dealing with background-versus-texture rather than nearness-to-focus. Instead of working outward from the focus, we scan the entire row and look at adjacent depth columns. The constrained columns are computed exactly the same way.

```
for (icol=0 ; icol<oversamp*nc-1 ; icol++) {
   icp1 = icol + 1 ;          // We now have a pair of adjacent columns: icol and icp1

   // If both columns are background, nothing to do ;
   if (txtptr[3*(icol/oversamp)+0] == bg_b  &&  txtptr[3*(icol/oversamp)+1] == bg_g  &&
       txtptr[3*(icol/oversamp)+2] == bg_r  &&   txtptr[3*(icp1/oversamp)+0] == bg_b  &&
       txtptr[3*(icp1/oversamp)+1] == bg_g  &&  txtptr[3*(icp1/oversamp)+2] == bg_r)
      continue ;

   // Left column in this adjacent pair
   z = row_depth[icol] ;
   idist = (int) ((1.0 - mu * z) / (2.0 - mu * z) * oversamp * eye + 0.5) ;
   icolL = icol - idist / 2 ;  // These are the columns originally used for constraining
   icolR = icolL + idist ;

   // Right column in this adjacent pair
   z = row_depth[icp1] ;
   idist = (int) ((1.0 - mu * z) / (2.0 - mu * z) * oversamp * eye + 0.5) ;
   icp1L = icp1 - idist / 2 ;  // These are the columns originally used for constraining
   icp1R = icp1L + idist ;
```

First we handle a gap in the left constrained columns. Order the endpoints correctly.

```
   icolL = (icolL >= 0) ? icolL : 0 ;
   icp1L = (icp1L >= 0) ? icp1L : 0 ;
   if (icolL < icp1L) {
      istart = icolL + 1 ;  // These are the skipped columns now subject to revision
      istop = icp1L - 1 ;
      }
   else {
      istart = icp1L + 1 ;
      istop = icolL - 1 ;
      }
```

Get the constraint class of the 'left' constrained column for the icol and the adjacent icol+1 columns. As in the sprite version, we require that both ends be constrained and at least one skipped column lies between them. We also prevent creating blocks of identical pixels, as in the sprite version.

```
cc_icol = constraint_class[icolL] ;
cc_icp1 = constraint_class[icp1L] ;
ok_to_postproc = 0 ;
if (istop >= istart  &&  cc_icol >= 0  &&  cc_icp1 >= 0) {      // This is the basic constraint
  ok_to_postproc = 1 ;
  if (istop - istart + 1 > oversamp)                            // Prevent occasional huge ugly blotches
    ok_to_postproc = 0 ;                                        // Sufficient oversampling will make this always false
}
```

Decide which endpoint (icol or icp1) will be copied. If one is texture and the other is not, we choose the texture. Otherwise we choose the closer (greater Z).

```
if (ok_to_postproc) {
  if (colormap[cc_icol].is_texture  &&  colormap[cc_icp1].is_texture) { // Both are texture, so break tie with Z
    if (colormap[cc_icol].Z > colormap[cc_icp1].Z)
      cc_copied = cc_icol ;
    else
      cc_copied = cc_icp1 ;
  }
  else if (colormap[cc_icol].is_texture)
    cc_copied = cc_icol ;
  else
    cc_copied = cc_icp1 ;
```

The last step is to loop through the skipped columns. For each, in the unusual situation that it is not yet constrained we create a new constraint class for it. Then copy the color, depth, and is_texture flag of the chosen endpoint.

```
for (i=istart ; i<=istop ; i++) {
  if (constraint_class[i] < 0) {          // Still unconstrained? (fairly unusual)
    constraint_class[i] = ncolors++ ;     // Give it its own new constraint class
  }

  k = constraint_class[i] ;
  colormap[k].r = colormap[cc_copied].r ;
  colormap[k].g = colormap[cc_copied].g ;
  colormap[k].b = colormap[cc_copied].b ;
  colormap[k].Z = colormap[cc_copied].Z ;
  colormap[k].is_texture = colormap[cc_copied].is_texture ;
  }
}
```

The right side is handled exactly as the left side was, so there is no need to walk through that code here.

Final color assignment is similar to how it was done in the sprite version. However, we have one simplification and one complexification to consider in this texture-mapped version:

- In the sprite version, unconstrained columns presented a quandary, with different developers choosing different solutions, none of which are ideal. It's easy in the texture-mapped version: unconstrained points are set to the background color, which is pure black in the *Stereo* program.

- When we average oversampled pixels to compute the final color of each stereogram pixel, we must not include background pixels in the average.

The optional median filters are applied exactly as was done in the sprite version, and multi-threading is also done the same way.

7

The Multiple-Object Stereogram Algorithm

The geometry and key equations for the multiple-object stereogram are identical to what we've seen in the prior two chapters, the basic operations are the same, and much of the code is identical. However, the algorithm is much simpler in one regard: we don't have to deal with four merging possibilities. This is because every instance of the object across the stereogram has an identical depth profile. So for any column in the depth and texture images, the spacing of the constrained columns in the stereogram is equal across the entire extent of the stereogram. Thus, we just march across at this spacing, setting pixel colors and combining constraint classes whenever needed.

The Mapping structure is the same as in the single-object stereogram, even though at this time the is_texture member is never used, though it is set for possible future use. The calling parameter list is essentially identical to what we've seen before, with one minor exception. Instead of passing the row number as a parameter (which is needed only if you want to insert debugging statements), I make it a global. I must have had tea instead of coffee that morning. This is of no practical consequence whatsoever, since the row number is made available for optional study or debugging only.

```
static void make_3d_3_worker (
    int nc ,                        // Number of columns in depth and output images
    int texture_bytes ,             // Bytes-per-pixel in texture and output (1 or 3)
    int depth_bytes ,               // Bytes-per-pixel in depth (1 or 3)
    unsigned char *txtptr ,         // Input single row in texture image
    unsigned char *depptr ,         // Input single row in depth image
    unsigned char *rowptr ,         // Output single row of stereo image
    int oversamp ,                  // Oversampling rate
    int *constraint_class ,         // Work array oversamp * nc long
    Mapping *colormap ,             // Work array oversamp * nc long
    double *row_depth ,             // Work array oversamp * nc long
    unsigned char *row_work         // Work array oversamp * nc * texture_bytes long
    )
```

We again fetch a few parameters from global storage. These could just as well be passed as parameters.

```
eye = stereo_params.eye_spacing ;    // These could be passed as parameters to avoid global reference
mu = stereo_params.mu ;
favor_Z = stereo_params.favor_Z ;

bg_r = bg_g = bg_b = (unsigned char) 0 ;   // Defined background color
```

We perform exactly the same initialization as with the single-image version. See the prior chapter for a detailed explanation if needed.

```
for (icol=0 ; icol<oversamp*nc ; icol++) {
   constraint_class[icol] = -1 ;  // Flag unconstrained
   ibase = icol / oversamp ;
   ijump = icol % oversamp ;
   if (stereo_params.interpz)
      frac = (double) ijump / (double) oversamp ;
   else
      frac = 0.0 ;
   if (depth_bytes == 1) {
      if (ibase == nc - 1)   // The last column cannot interpolate because there is no 'next' column
         row_depth[icol] = depptr[ibase] / 255.0 ;
      else
         row_depth[icol] = (depptr[ibase] + frac * (depptr[ibase+1] - depptr[ibase])) / 255.0 ;
      }
   else if (depth_bytes == 3) {
      if (ibase == nc - 1)
         row_depth[icol] = (depptr[3*ibase] + depptr[3*ibase+1]) / (2.0 * 255.0) ;
      else {
         row_depth[icol]  = depptr[3*ibase+0] + frac * (depptr[3*(ibase+1)+0] - depptr[3*ibase+0]) ;
         row_depth[icol] += depptr[3*ibase+1] + frac * (depptr[3*(ibase+1)+1] - depptr[3*ibase+1]) ;
         row_depth[icol] /= 2.0 * 255.0 ;
         }
      }
   }

ncolors = 0 ;  // Counts colors in the colormap
```

The main outer loop just passes across the entire row, skipping columns that are background. For each non-background column, it begins just like the single-object version: it computes the distance separating constrained columns (idist) and then checks to see if the current column is hidden by a part of the object that is closer to the observer. If either eye is obscured, it skips processing and moves on to the next column. See the prior chapter if you would like a detailed discussion of this next large block of code.

```
for (icol=0 ; icol<oversamp*nc ; icol++) {     // For every column of depth and output, process only texture

   if (texture_bytes == 1) {
      texture_b = txtptr[icol/oversamp] ;
      if (texture_b == bg_b)                    // Is this column background?
         continue ;                             // If so, nothing to do
      }

   else if (texture_bytes == 3) {
      texture_b = txtptr[3*(icol/oversamp)+0] ;          // Blue
      texture_g = txtptr[3*(icol/oversamp)+1] ;          // Green
      texture_r = txtptr[3*(icol/oversamp)+2] ;          // Red
      if (texture_b == bg_b  &&  texture_g == bg_g  &&  texture_r == bg_r)     // Is this column background?
         continue ;                                                           // If so, nothing to do
      }

   z = row_depth[icol] ;
   idist = (int) ((1.0 - mu * z) / (2.0 - mu * z) * oversamp * eye + 0.5) ;

   left = icol - idist / 2 ;           // Split the distance into left and right
   if (left < 0)                       // If left eye's view is outside the view
      continue ;                       // Nothing more to do

   right = left + idist ;              // This point will be constrained: same as left
   if (right >= oversamp * nc)         // If we are outside the image
      continue ;                       // Nothing more to do

   k = 1 ;                             // Check this far on each side of this point
   factor = 2.0 * (2.0 - mu * z) / (mu * oversamp * eye) ; // Slope of line
   hidden = 0 ;

   for (;;) {                          // Loop until hidden status is determined
      zk = z + k * factor ;            // Move along the line of sight
      if (zk >= 1.0)                   // Upper limit, so it can't be hidden
         break ;
      if ((icol >= k)  &&  (row_depth[icol-k] >= zk)) { // Left eye
         hidden = 1 ;                  // If this neighbor pt is in front of line of sight
         break ;
         }
```

```
    if ((icol + k < oversamp * nc)  &&  (row_depth[icol+k] >= zk)) {
      hidden = 1 ;
      break ;
      }
    ++k ;          // Keep checking, moving further from point
    }


  // If either eye is hidden (or both, which happens at a deep ravine)
  // then we will not be linking these left and right viewplane columns.

  if (hidden)
    continue ; // Skip over left-right constraining code
```

When we get here, we know that the object at column icol is not hidden and must be processed. We create a new color map entry for it. There is no need for the is_texture member of the Mapping structure, because at this time all color maps are texture. Feel free to eliminate all references to it. I put it here to facilitate a future use for this flag, much as was done in the single-object version.

Also note that, as will be seen in the next code block, in some circumstances we will not need this new color map. Sometimes there may be an existing constraint class for this column. We will then stick with the existing constraint class, possibly modified. It's easier and more clear to just create it, even if occasionally we will not need it.

```
  colormap[ncolors].is_texture = 1 ;   // Not needed because ALL colormap entries are for texture
  colormap[ncolors].n_texture = 1 ;    // Ditto if we always favor Z
  colormap[ncolors].Z = row_depth[icol] ;

  colormap[ncolors].b = texture_b ;
  if (texture_bytes == 3) {
    colormap[ncolors].g = texture_g ;
    colormap[ncolors].r = texture_r ;
    }

  ++ncolors ;
```

This next code block, the core component of the algorithm, is very different from the sprite and single-object versions. This difference arises from the fact that every instance of the object has the same depth. As a result, for any column in the depth and texture images, the distance separating constrained columns is exactly the same across the entire stereogram. Thus, for any column we simply compute idist and then constrain all columns across the stereogram that are spaced at this distance. The color we use is determined by the pixel at icol, offset as usual by idist/2. The leftmost constrained column is at left%idist, and we will move to the right in jumps of idist until we would pass the end of the image. Most of the time, the column to be constrained will be unconstrained when we get there, so we just assign it to the color map just created and move on.

```
for (j=left%idist ; j<oversamp*nc ; j+=idist) {
  ccl = constraint_class[j] ;   // Class of pixel seen by left eye

  if (ccl < 0) {  // Unconstrained, most common situation
    constraint_class[j] = ncolors - 1 ;   // Color map just created for this texture pixel
    continue ;
    }
```

But occasionally we will find that the column we are about to constrain is already constrained. This happens when the depth changes to a degree that exactly matches and offsets the change in icol. In this situation we act according to whether the user has requested favoring Z (usually bad) versus averaging (usually good). If averaging is requested, we compute a weighted average of the current color and the color of icol.

```
if (! favor_Z) {
  colormap[ccl].Z = (row_depth[icol] > colormap[ccl].Z) ? row_depth[icol] : colormap[ccl].Z ;
  colormap[ccl].b = (unsigned char) ((colormap[ccl].n_texture * colormap[ccl].b + texture_b) /
                                    (colormap[ccl].n_texture + 1.0)) ;
  if (texture_bytes == 3) {
    colormap[ccl].g = (unsigned char) ((colormap[ccl].n_texture * colormap[ccl].g + texture_g) /
                                    (colormap[ccl].n_texture + 1.0)) ;
    colormap[ccl].r = (unsigned char) ((colormap[ccl].n_texture * colormap[ccl].r + texture_r) /
                                    (colormap[ccl].n_texture + 1.0)) ;
    }
  ++colormap[ccl].n_texture ;
  }
```

If, on the other hand, the user has requested favoring Z, we compare the depth at icol with the depth of the pixel that determined the currently constrained color. If the current pixel is closer to the observer than the prior pixel, we reset the existing color map to reflect the pixel at icol. Once again, recall that our setting of is_texture here is not needed because this member is always ignored in the current version of the algorithm. It's there to prepare for a more advanced version of the algorithm not yet implemented. Omit it if you wish.

```
    else if (row_depth[icol] > colormap[ccl].Z) {        // Closer?
      colormap[ccl].n_texture = 1 ;
      colormap[ccl].is_texture = 1 ;                      // Not needed because ALL colormaps are texture
      colormap[ccl].Z = row_depth[icol] ;
      colormap[ccl].b = texture_b ;
      if (texture_bytes == 3) {
        colormap[ccl].g = texture_g ;
        colormap[ccl].r = texture_r ;
        }
      } // If closer
    } // For j
  } // For icol
```

The next step is optionally fixing hidden pixel problems. The algorithm here is identical to that for the single-object version, so I'll omit it from this discussion. See the prior chapter for details.

The final step in color map assignment is to fix problems with stereogram columns being skipped due to rapid depth changes. The idea behind what we do here is exactly the same as that for the single-object version, so it would be good to review that discussion in the prior chapter before proceeding. However, the exact implementation here is considerably simpler than that for the single-object version, again because constrained-column spacing in this version is equal across the stereogram for any source pixel. We don't need to worry about both left and right constrained columns for a value of icol. Instead, we just march across the texture/depth images, examining all adjacent pairs of columns and compute the corresponding two values of idist that will be the common value for the entire row.

```
  for (icol=0 ; icol<oversamp*nc-1 ; icol++) {
    icp1 = icol + 1 ;
```

If either column is background, there is nothing to do. Both columns must be texture in order for it to make sense to proceed.

```
if ((txtptr[3*(icol/oversamp)+0] == bg_b && txtptr[3*(icol/oversamp)+1] == bg_g  && txtptr[3*(icol/oversamp)+2] == bg_r)
  || (txtptr[3*(icp1/oversamp)+0] == bg_b && txtptr[3*(icp1/oversamp)+1] == bg_g && txtptr[3*(icp1/oversamp)+2] == bg_r))
    continue ;
```

We need to look only at the left constrained column (or only the right for a trivially different version of the algorithm) because the spacing is equal for every instance. For the variable names here, 'left' and 'right' refer to icol and icp1, the left and right source columns in the adjacent pair. Compute these left-constrained columns for each adjacent point. Then walk them to the left in constraint-sized jumps until either or both of them become negative. This provides the starting point for moving across the stereogram in equal jumps.

```
// Left column in this adjacent pair
z = row_depth[icol] ;
idist_col = (int) ((1.0 - mu * z) / (2.0 - mu * z) * oversamp * eye + 0.5) ;
icolL = icol - idist_col / 2 ;              // These are the columns originally used for constraining

// Right column in this adjacent pair
z = row_depth[icp1] ;
idist_cp1 = (int) ((1.0 - mu * z) / (2.0 - mu * z) * oversamp * eye + 0.5) ;
icp1L = icp1 - idist_cp1 / 2 ;              // These are the columns originally used for constraining

while (icolL >= 0  &&  icp1L >= 0) {        // Get starting point for left-to-right run
  icolL -= idist_col ;
  icp1L -= idist_cp1 ;
  }
```

The loop that marches across the image for this icol/icp1 pair takes jumps that, for each of the two adjacent columns, are equal. Of course, it will often be the case (when icol and icp1 have different depths) that these distances will be different from each other. Stop when we are about to pass the end of the row.

```
for (;;) {                    // Process every repetition instance due to this pair of texture columns
  icolL += idist_col ;      // We start with both of them inside the image
  icp1L += idist_cp1 ;
  if (icolL >= oversamp*nc  ||  icp1L >= oversamp*nc)
    break ;
```

As we have done in the other stereogram algorithms, we must make sure that the starting and stopping columns for the remapping are ordered. Also, be absolutely sure that they are legally bounded.

```
if (icolL < icp1L) {
   istart = icolL + 1 ;  // These are the skipped columns now subject to revision
   istop = icp1L - 1 ;
   }
else {
   istart = icp1L + 1 ;
   istop = icolL - 1 ;
   }

if (istart < 0)
   istart = 0 ;
if (istop < 0)
   istop = 0 ;

if (istop >= oversamp*nc)
   istop = oversamp*nc - 1 ;
```

Get the constraint class of each of these columns. Note that they may be –1 (unconstrained) if icol was a hidden pixel. Then decide if we should remap these skipped columns. The basic requirement is that there be at least one skipped column, and that both ends be constrained to some color. Also, we prevent remapping blocks of pixels to the same color, which is ugly in normal (and perhaps 3D) vision. This is discussed in the prior chapter. Recall that sufficiently large oversampling will always cause that 'if' statement to fail, meaning that any harm (black speckles) caused by this test can be overcome by oversampling.

```
cc_icol = constraint_class[icolL] ;
cc_icp1 = constraint_class[icp1L] ;

ok_to_postproc = 0 ;

if (istop >= istart  &&  cc_icol >= 0  &&  cc_icp1 >= 0) {    // This is the basic requirement
   ok_to_postproc = 1 ;
   if (istop - istart + 1 > oversamp)                        // Prevent occasional huge ugly blotches
     ok_to_postproc = 0 ;                                    // Sufficient oversampling will make this always false
```

If both ends of the skipped region are the same color, it's pretty much a no-brainer to color everything skipped to be the same color. I suppose that, in theory, this could cause ugliness in some pathological situations, but I've never seen it happen, and this catch can sometimes prevent the need for extreme oversampling to overcome the blotch test. If you don't like this 'no-brainer' test, feel free to omit it.

```
// This is a no-brainer: both ends same color
if (texture_bytes == 1) {
   if (colormap[cc_icol].b == colormap[cc_icp1].b)
      ok_to_postproc = 1 ;
   }
else if (texture_bytes == 3) {
   if (colormap[cc_icol].r == colormap[cc_icp1].r  &&  colormap[cc_icol].g == colormap[cc_icp1].g  &&
       colormap[cc_icol].b == colormap[cc_icp1].b)
      ok_to_postproc = 1 ;
   }
}
```

If we are to remap the skipped columns, do so now. The color is determined by whichever endpoint is closer to the observer, with the thought that it is less likely to be hidden. Naturally, if some column that was skipped for this icol column is already mapped due to some other source column, don't mess with it.

```
if (ok_to_postproc) {
   if (colormap[cc_icol].Z > colormap[cc_icp1].Z)
      cc_copied = cc_icol ;
   else
      cc_copied = cc_icp1 ;

   for (i=istart ; i<=istop ; i++) {
      if (constraint_class[i] < 0)
         constraint_class[i] = cc_copied ;
      }
   } // If ok_to_postproc
 } // Endless for loop
} // For icol
```

The remainder of this code (color assignment, oversampling, median filtering) is identical to what we saw in the prior chapter, so we'll dispense with further discussion.

8

Depth Images with Blender

If you are serious about designing or editing existing 3D graphics, especially for the purpose of creating stereograms, you would be well advised to learn to use Blender. This is an astonishingly powerful program, all the more astonishing because it is free. One of its great advantages for stereogram artistry is that Blender makes it easy to simultaneously create texture maps and depth images that are precisely aligned, pixel by pixel. It is also easy to make these images have a pure black background, which is exactly what the *Stereo* program requires.

By way of warning, I will comment on one downside of Blender, just to prepare readers lest they be surprised. And please, all you Blender experts, don't hate me for this; everyone is entitled to their opinion. My opinion (from much experience!) is that the learning curve for Blender is somewhat steeper than Mount Everest. This is partly because of the mind-boggling power of the program. It can do so many, many things that deciding on the best way to do what you want to do can itself be a daunting task. And then of course you have to ignore everything else. I studied and seriously used the program for many months, and I can definitely say that I know just a couple percent of what it can do. There are so many capabilities built into the program that ignoring the things that have nothing to do with your task is surprisingly difficult.

The other warning I have about Blender, directed at those who have never used it, is that for some reason my intuition about how things should work is often in severe conflict with the designers' intuition. When I want to select an object, I intuitively click on it with the left mouse button. In Blender, you click on things with the right mouse button to select them (unless you laboriously change defaults). The screen tends to fill with windows that you don't want or need, but getting rid of them reminds me of the Sorcerer's Apprentice scene in Fantasia. You do what your intuition tells you is the way to get rid of the window, and suddenly you have two of them! So you cuss a little, think you made a mistake, and very slowly and carefully attempt to get rid of the window again. Shazam, you now have three of them! Blender is like that. You *cannot* learn it quickly on your own, because so much of it is counterintuitive. You have to go to YouTube and work through tutorials. I even paid to join a Blender Artists professional community where I could watch very well created tutorial videos, generally higher quality than can be found on YouTube. The reason I'm making such a big deal of this is that I do not want beginners to install the program, play with it a little, and get discouraged and quit. Help is available. Swallow hard and get to work watching videos of experts. Honestly, I believe that is the only way to learn this amazing program.

I suggest that you investigate cgtrader.com. Talented Blender artists post their works to sell, usually at prices that are more than fair and without onerous copyright restrictions. Most examples in this book came from this site, and it is always easiest to start with an expertly crafted model and then tweak it as needed.

Creating Texture and Depth Files

This is not the place to offer a full tutorial on Blender, so this section will assume that you are already familiar with the basics of the program. I cover only the specific steps needed to produce texture and depth images suitable for import into *Stereo*.

Figure 60 below shows the Compositing view in Blender using the Cycles rendering engine. At the right side you see that I have selected the *Background* surface, defined it as RGB, and set that color to pure black. This provides the black background *Stereo* needs for the texture map. Near the center of this figure, observe that *Use Nodes* has been checked so that the node window displays the compositing data flow. Also, *Backdrop* has been checked so that the viewer node's feed is displayed in the center of this screen. I always make this the depth image. Figure 61 on the next page is a closeup of the nodes display.

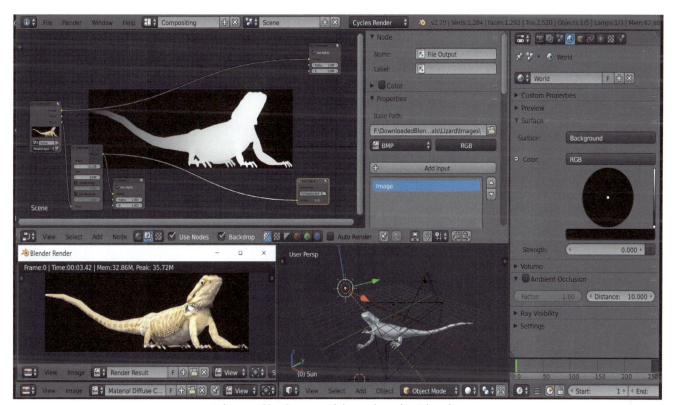

Figure 60: Compositing view in Blender

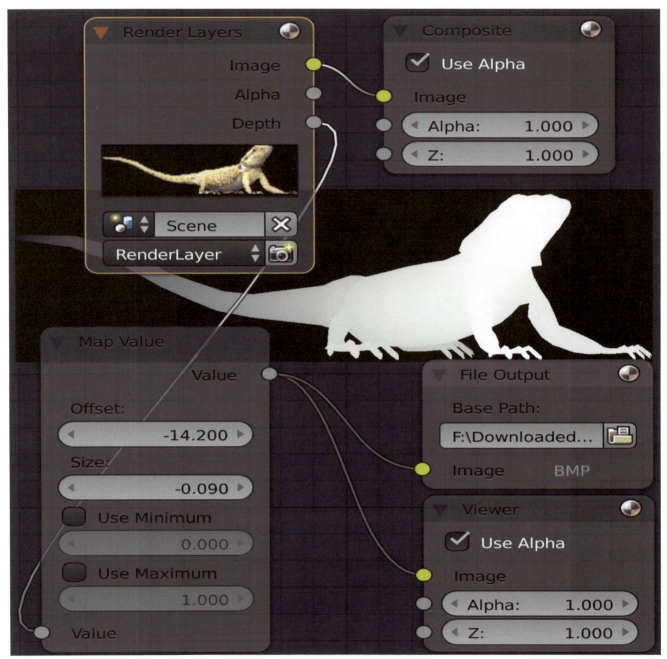

Figure 61: Node display in Blender

The first thing you need to do is add a Vector / Map Value node. Connect its input to the Depth output from the Render Layers node. This is the distance between each point on the model and the camera. Connect the output of the Map Value node to a viewer node so the depth image appears in the backdrop. The Z value increases as the distance between the object and the camera decreases, the opposite of the Depth output, so you need a negative multiplier. You also need to offset the distance so that it scales correctly.

A lot of trial and error is needed at this point. Adjust the scale (Size field) and offset so that the range of the depth image covers as well as possible the full range from black to white, without saturating at the white end, which would result in a big flat area at the front of the object. Some artists scale up the object to extremely large size, in which case tweaking the scale and offset is a lot easier if you add a second Map Value node in the path, with the first node doing the bulk of the scale/offset work, and the second being used for fine tuning. In such cases, that's a lot easier than tweaking by changing a number in the fourth decimal place!

Once you have it tweaked as well as possible, you can add a File Output node. Be sure to set the file type to BMP. Twiddle with the row and column dimensions so that your object is nicely framed. You can always correct things later in *Stereo*, but you might as well get close to the final size now. You would do well to perform some final fine tuning of the scale and offset by generating trial images and checking pixel values in an external image editor.

To output a texture file, just feed the File Output node from the Image output of the Render Layers node, instead of the scaled depth. You'll soon discover that Blender has some counter-intuitive rules for naming and placing files, so whenever you have the 'perfect' file you would be well advised to rename it and move it to a safe place so that it does not get overwritten!

It has been my experience that Blender does an excellent job of producing these files. They are clean and clear. Moreover, and of particular importance to *Stereo*, the texture and depth images are perfectly registered, right down to the pixel level. Once you get past the initial intimidation of learning to use this daunting program, you will be amazed at how perfect it is for building, editing, and writing files for elaborate 3D models. I could not have produced this book without it.

www.ingramcontent.com/pod-product-compliance
Lightning Source LLC
Chambersburg PA
CBHW041429050326
40690CB00002B/473